AS LONG AS YOU LOVE THEM

Do you know:

BRIAN's worst habit? (he bites his fing...

A.J.'s favorite food?

NICK's favorite s...

KEVIN's confessi...

HOWIE's trade se...   ...o keep
  his vocal chords...

FIND OUT MORE ABOUT YOUR
FAVE GROUP, THE MEGA-HOT
BACKSTREET BOYS!

Backstreet
BOYS

Anna Louise Golden

St. Martin's Paperbacks

BACKSTREET BOYS

Copyright © 1998 by Anna Louise Golden.

Cover photograph © Bob Berg/Retna Ltd. USA.

ISBN: 0-312-96853-1

Printed in the United States of America

St. Martin's Paperbacks edition / June 1998

St. Martin's Paperbacks are published by St. Martin's Press, 175 Fifth Avenue, New York, NY 10010.

10 9 8 7 6 5 4 3 2 1

FOR BLAIR

ACKNOWLEDGMENTS

As always, my agent, Madeleine Morel, thank you so very, very much. At St. Martin's I'm indebted to Glenda Howard and John Rounds, for belief in an idea. My parents, Jonathon and Judy Savill, Mike Murtagh, Dennis Wilken, Paul Clark, and those all over—you know who you are—whose support is and always will be invaluable to me. The very helpful people at Soundwaves in Seattle, and at A&B Sound in Vancouver, B.C., especially Meghan Banks, who honestly couldn't have done more if she'd owed me money. This book would be a lesser thing without you all.

Bop, BB, Teen Machine, Lime, Entertainment Weekly, Teen People, Los Angeles Times, and *Top of the Pops* magazine were all source material in researching this book. There were other articles where I was unable to locate an original source—if those people would like to contact me, full credit can be given in any future editions.

INTRODUCTION

It used to be that people came to Florida for the heat. These days it's the heat from Florida that's going all over the world—the Backstreet Boys.

They call Florida the Sunshine State, but Nick, Brian, Kevin, Howie, and AJ are taking that sunshine around the globe, a bigger export even than the oranges that Florida is famous for.

It's an irresistible sound—the mixture of harmony and beat—the kind that's fueled pop dreams for decades. The boy bands have always been a part of pop music, going back to the doo-wop of the Fifties, where guys would gather on the street corners and sing in harmony. In the Seventies it was the Jackson Five (where a very young Michael had his start) and the Osmonds who rode the chart wave, and in the early Nineties New Kids On The Block and New Edition—the starting place for Bobby Brown—sold records and stole hearts.

For so long it seemed that the boy band was a very American phenomenon. America, with its tradition of harmony singing, did it best. But by the mid-Nineties, the Brits were pushing at the turf. Boyzone, 3T, East 17, and the phenomenally successful Take That all laid claim to the title of top boy band. But once the BSB opened their mouths, it was all over for everyone else. Each of them had their strengths, but once you put them all together, they became unstoppable!

From the moment Nick, AJ, and Howie started singing together, there was magic in their voices, and once they teamed up with Brian and Kevin, it was obvious that stardom was going to be the next stop.

If there was one surprise about the journey to the top, though, it was that it began in Europe, rather than back home in the U.S. But boy bands were happening there, while America really didn't seem to know what it was looking for.

It all began with the songs they recorded at the beginning of 1995, going to Sweden to work with producer Denniz PoP, then back home in Florida to release their first single and the *Backstreet Boys* album.

They had the material, they—and everybody else who heard them—were stoked about the group, and now they had to take it on the road. ''We've Got It Goin' Out'' was the first single, released simultaneously in America and Europe. Although it didn't do too well at home, only rising to #69 on the chart, it took off like a rocket in Germany, all the way to the Top Ten. So the band was on its way, performing in Germany, and in England, where the band's live appearances were enough to create a storm (although the single only rose to #54; re-released ten months later, the same song would shoot all the way up to #3!). All of a sudden they had fans going wild for them. In Britain they opened for PJ and Duncan, bringing down the house every night with their looks and their voices. This was a band that just couldn't be ignored, and they weren't—*Smash Hits*' readers went out and voted them Best Newcomers of the Year, a huge boost and vote of confidence for the Boys.

The next single, ''Get Down (You're The One For Me)'' showed them making real progress to the top, as it peaked at #14 in England, and did even better in other countries throughout Europe, including their first German Number One. But Canada was also taking notice. What was happening there was virtually Backstreet mania! Their records were selling like proverbial hotcakes, and they were on their way!

Throughout the summer and fall of 1996 things just got better and better. Instead of being the newcomers, the Backstreet Boys were now the ones to beat, *the* boy band. They'd spent the spring making their album, and now they were ready to unleash it on the world.

Backstreet Boys had barely been released in Germany before it went platinum. Canada sent it triple platinum. In Spain they were mobbed by hordes of fans, pulling the clothes and jewelry from their bodies. It was unlike anything they'd ever known or expected. Without even trying, just by singing and being themselves, the Backstreet Boys were a genuine phenomenon.

"We did this live show at this radio station in Spain and when we came out, we were mobbed," recalls Kevin. "I had a necklace on that meant a great deal to me—my brother gave it to me one Christmas—and this girl just ripped it off my neck."

But adoring fans were something the Boys would have to get used to. Not only in Europe, but all over the world. Throughout Asia, people loved them, in India, the Philippines, Australia, Singapore, Malaysia.

The one place that seemed slow to catch up was America. But that would all change in due course. By the time they came home, they were already megastars everywhere else.

But it wasn't until 1997 that things started to jump for BSB in the U.S. Even then, things were a little different. The *Backstreet Boys* album that appeared in the States wasn't the same as their debut of that title elsewhere. The rest of the world had just received their second taste of BSB, in the form of the *Backstreet's Back* album. The American *Backstreet Boys* record mixed and matched songs from both those releases onto one disc.

Why? Well, the Boys might have been American homies, but the U.S. had just too much catching up to do. There was no way BSB could have put out two albums at once. This just caught them at their *very* best.

As soon as it had the chance, America understood why everyone else loved the BSB so much, and got with it. Ahead of the album, ''Quit Playing Games (With My Heart)'' appeared, and immediately made the Backstreet Boys into stars, rising all the way to #2, and spending more than nine months in the Top Fifty, going platinum—one million copies sold—in the process.

Backstreet Boys would repeat the process, going all the way to #4 in the album charts, and doubling that magical million mark, logging a full half year and counting as a best-seller.

America was a year behind everyone else, but they'd finally caught on. BSB were a massive international success story. The male media might have been tightly focused on the Spice Girls, but BSB were right up there with them, with four Top Ten singles around the globe, and a debut album that had gone gold, platinum, or multiplatinum in a staggering *thirty-five* countries! And how did that translate into sales? Try eleven million albums.

And in July 1997, within a week of its release worldwide (except the U.S., of course), the single ''Everybody (Backstreet's Back)'' was in the Top Ten in ten countries.

But that was only to be expected from the band that won the Select MTV Europe Music Award at the end of 1996. Decided by viewers, and presented to the band by former Take That heartthrob Robbie Williams, it reflected just how popular the band had become. And just to prove it wasn't luck, they won it again at the end of 1997!

It was time to bring it all back home, a place they'd hardly had time to see for the last two years. And with a massive single and album, they were doing it all in style.

''We haven't been home for Thanksgiving for three

years," Nick says. ". . . Last year we were staying in Britain and it was really great, but there's nothing like homemade pumpkin pie!"

And America was certainly crazy for them.

"It's great to have recognition at home," Brian admits. "It took a long time, but finally our fellow Americans have cottoned onto us." And he feels that the success of the Spice Girls had helped pave the way for them. "I think a lot of it has to do with the Spice Girls bringing pop back into the U.S. They started getting successful and everybody in America turned round and said, 'Okay, where are the homegrown acts?' So we turned up and said, 'Here we are. We've been here all along, you just never noticed before.' "

They were certainly sitting up and paying attention now. From Florida to the world, and now back home again, BSB had it *all* going for them. A North American trek in January and February of 1998 saw them covering the continent, selling out venues like the 27,000 seat Skydome in Toronto, before capping it all off with a real final homecoming at the House of Blues in Orlando—which also sold out as soon as tickets were announced—and packing their passports for three more months in Europe, with dates in France, Ireland, England, all over Scandinavia, Holland, Belgium, and Spain.

Then, finally, they'd be back home for a while and receiving what would be almost the ultimate accolade—playing five nights, over the course of two weeks—at the Magic Kingdom, in Orlando, for Grad nights, meaning some lucky seniors would pack a lifetime of memories into a single evening.

Never mind the looks—although all five are absolutely gorgeous—these are five guys with what it takes. Talent, they say, will out, and in the case of the Backstreet Boys, there was no way it could be denied, particularly for Nick, the youngest of the crew.

"Sometimes [people] do get the wrong impression," he says, " 'cause all they see is the young, blond boy thing, but it makes me want to show them what I'm really like even more. And I think that's what Backstreet Boys is all about—being ourselves. There are times when you're out and guys got something to say to you, but you just take it all with a grain of salt."

The key to it all is that they're a *group*. They're friends. Howie, Kev, and Brain even share an apartment in Orlando, close to Universal studios, although they rarely get to spend any time there these days.

"Communication is the biggest key to keeping everything together," Howie explains. "We are like blood brothers and like any family, we have our ups and downs. In fact, we're together twenty-four hours a day, seven days a week. So communication is important. We don't keep things inside us and then blow up one day. We talk freely and try to do things that are for the good of the group."

And they plan on keeping everything together.

"I don't think any of us are thinking about going solo," AJ says. "It's like the whole New Edition thing that's going on: somewhere down the line we could all go solo, but then we'd get back together ten years later and be even better than we were before!"

The way things are going, there's no reason they'd ever want to break up. They've worked hard for their success, to win their fans. All over the world people are buying their records, putting their posters on their walls, watching their videos. But none of it has gone to their heads, according to Brian.

"I hope the success never stops," he admits. "I want us to be around for a long time, but you have to take it step by step, day by day, dealing with things that come your way in a logical manner. It's so easy to fall into your own hype."

And that's never going to happen. They're five guys

with their feet very firmly planted on the ground. They're still astonished by everything that's happened, and, being genuinely *nice* guys, they appreciate their fans.

"We're really focused on not taking our fans for granted," AJ explains. "You can't get caught up with it, because there is no way to please everybody. But when we can, we like to give them some special attention. We're just trying to be nice and give them a little something back."

"We've got some brilliant fans," Brian adds. "We get really excited when we're flying back into a country like Britain, because we get to meet them again—we literally sit on the plane going, 'Oh, do you think Helen, or Louise, or whoever, will be at the airport?'"

Sometimes the good guys really do win, and the Backstreet Boys are definitely the good guys. The best guys. But who are Kev, AJ, Brian, Howie, and Nick? How did the band get together . . . and just what is it that makes them so special?

♪ *PART ONE* ♪

THE BOYS

Like any band, the guys in the Backstreet Boys are all individuals. They come from different backgrounds, different circumstances, different parts of the U.S. But when they get together, between them they have some magical ingredients. Not only could they harmonize—and if anyone thinks they can't sing, hear them go at it a capella on a radio show sometime!—but they have something very few possess. Call it charisma, star quality, anything you want, but BSB have it to spare.

Anyone who's been lucky enough to see them in concert, or who's bought their concert video, also knows that these five can *move*. The dancing is as much a part of the show as the singing, but it's more than a step here and a step there. They Boys have some complicated routines, absolutely precise and demanding.

"I remember once we were performing a song from the album on stage," Brian recalls, "and I had to sing the first two verses. The dance routine was really difficult and I was concentrating so hard I blanked on the words. I ended up just humming along. The other guys were useless. They were creased up laughing and didn't try to help me out at all."

Still, they got through it all. Together, they've got through a lot. They look out for each other. For Kev, it's like having four younger brothers around (although maybe not quite as annoying), and for Nick the band replaces the family he misses so much when he's out on the road—which seems like most of the time now.

If there are problems, they talk them through. They've been around each other long enough to know that's the only solution. Otherwise arguments start, bad feelings occur, and no one's happy. It helps that they genuinely like each other—why else would Kev, Brian, and Howie share an apartment when they can all afford their own houses?—but they're also genuine, considerate people.

They got into all this because it was what they *wanted* to do. BSB aren't a manufactured group. AJ, Nick, and Howie were singing together long before there was any sort of success. They did it because they loved music and loved to sing. And when Kevin joined, and then Brian, they had exactly the right balance of voices and harmonies. But they're still doing it for the same reasons—that love of music and singing. It's just that instead of entertaining themselves, these days they're doing it for thousands of people at each show.

But the Backstreet Boys are five very different guys, all of whom bring very different things to the band. Find out about each of them, and you'll begin to get an idea of what makes Backstreet tick. . . .

♪ **KEV** ♪

Kentucky is a state of contrasts. To the east, by the West Virginia border, it's still hard times, where the coal mines have closed, with nothing to replace them, and the Appalachian traditions still live on. Head west, toward Lexington and Louisville, and you reach the Kentucky that everyone hears about, the rich bluegrass, the white-painted fences, and the horse farms.

Colonel Sanders and his world-famous Kentucky Fried Chicken got their start in this area, still in the South, but so close to Cincinnati and the industry of the North. It's where the two cultures seem to meet. Country stores have Kentucky hams hanging from the beams, the sense of Southern hospitality fills the air, and there's a slightly slower pace of life, but at the same time, the rest of the world never seems too far away.

This is where Kevin Scott Richardson was born on March 10, 1972. His parents, Anne and Jerald Wayne Richardson, already had two boys, Jerald, Jr., age six, and Timothy, age three, and Kevin completed their family.

Jerald, Sr. was a big, athletic man who loved the outdoors, and was very handy—he could fix anything around the house. He and Anne had been high-school sweethearts, marrying not long after graduation. After the first two boys were born, the family had moved out of Lexington itself, into a more rural area, to live in a modern-day log cabin with a ten-acre farm around it. It was still close enough to the city to be accessible, but with plenty of fresh air and fewer neighbors around.

The family was musical—Kevin's grandfather had been a piano player and had sung in a barbershop quartet, but Kevin at first showed no inclination toward music himself. As a toddler he was extremely shy and self-contained, exploring around the family's property on his own—well, with his imaginary friend, Pixie.

Having two older brothers around kept him in line, but the age difference was such that Kevin didn't play with them much. In fact, he really didn't open up at all until he began kindergarten, when, according to his mom, he received the "Standing In The Corner Award," for causing trouble. Once he started first grade, the real Kevin began to peek through: talking all the time, even when the teacher was trying to run the class, which brought him the year's "Spanking Medal."

He also found a love of reading there.

"When I was little, I absolutely loved *The Cat In The Hat* books," he admits. The Dr. Seuss series, so loved by kids everywhere, really affected him, and made him into someone happy to hunker down with a book. Even today, he says, when the Boys are away on tour, "I always take books to read."

Once he'd begun to blossom, there was no stopping him! Kevin soon began to find a whole host of interests. Like his dad and his brothers, he was big, and soon began trying out for football and Little League, spending a lot of time practicing after school.

"I had a great childhood," he admits. "I loved school, played Little League, rode horses and dirtbikes." And like most kids, he even tried his hand at being a star, singing "into a hairbrush in front of my bedroom mirror."

Music initially came into his life through church.

"I grew up singing in church," he explains. "Me and

my mom—who's is Brian's father's sister—I sang duets with her in church.''

When he was nine, though, the family moved back into the city; country living wasn't all they'd expected, and his dad wanted to be closer to work. Kevin wasn't phased by the change, however. It just gave him a new set of kids to know and entertain.

By now he'd discovered drama, and began adding that to his singing in school. Music was slowly taking up more and more of his time, but he was also discovering girls!

''My first kiss was with a girl called Gina Davison who I went to school with.'' Kevin, who was ten then, had invited her out skating at the local ice rink, and it happened. ''I was in fifth grade. She was nice. That was my first real kiss.''

But not his last, by any means!

When he wasn't seeing Gina—and it didn't last long— all Kevin's free time was filled with homework, going to dances, the school football games, and just hanging with his friends. As if all that wasn't enough, he began taking part in local theatrical productions. With a natural love of musicals, he was soon finding roles in productions of ''Bye Bye Birdie'' and ''Barefoot in the Park.''

Seeing how interested Kevin was in music, and the way that Elton John's songs really seemed to capture his interest, when Kevin became a freshman in high school, Jerald and Anne bought him a keyboard. Learning to play wasn't as easy as he'd imagined, and he spent a lot of evenings and Sundays wrestling with it, learning chords and fills he could use to accompany his voice, which had only improved once it had *broken*.

He stayed very firmly involved with the chorus, but was also spending a lot of time in the drama club, taking part in school plays.

And the more he practiced, the better he became on the keyboards, until, after a year, when he finally felt ready to begin playing in front of people. Singing for an audience had never been a problem—by now it was almost second nature, as long as he was part of a chorus or a choir, and had others around him. But this was different. With just him and his keyboard, Kevin felt very alone.

Still, when they applauded, it felt great! It was possible to believe he was really like Elton or Billy Joel, the two artists whose songs he often performed, along with the Eagles and Prince.

"I really respect Elton John and Billy Joel and those guys—especially Prince, I think that Prince is a musical genius. He's played every instrument known to man."

One person who encouraged him was his cousin, Brian Littrell. Three years younger, he also loved to sing, and was almost as good as Kevin. He'd come over, and the two of them would harmonize as Kevin played.

Kevin really didn't know his young cousin that well, though.

"When we would have family outings," Brian recalls, "[Kevin] would always go hang out with my brother. It was like my brother and him were real tight, because they were the same age. I was the baby of the family . . ."

But although Brian's brother Harold Baker Littrell III (to give him his full name) and Kevin were friends, they didn't share quite the musical bond that Kev and Brian did. Kevin loved pop and R&B, and so did Brian.

Not that it stopped Kevin and Harold from having fun.

"They would get together and sing and pretend they were rock stars," Brian says, "and my brother would beat on the drums. My brother never took it seriously . . ."

Kevin did, though. Eventually he had a repertoire of songs and began playing in restaurants around the area. It wasn't exactly the greatest job in the world, providing background music while people ate, but it proved to be great training for him. He could try things and develop that singing voice of his! And it certainly beat bagging groceries in the supermarket or working at McDonald's.

That wasn't his only job. Kevin had developed a love of dancing, particularly ballroom dancing, and discovered he had a natural affinity for it. He was so good, in fact, that a local studio took him on as an instructor—just in case you ever wondered where his stage moves came from!

Of course, it ate into his time, particularly his nights, which meant that when the alarm went off, Kevin wasn't always ready for this day. As him mom recalls, her biggest problem with Kevin was "getting him up for school in the mornings."

He'd grown into a very good-looking teenager, one who was never short of a girlfriend for dances or parties—when he had the free time, of course!

Although he was very serious about music, and loved it, he knew it would be difficult to make a living from it. Playing piano in restaurants was a good way to make money when he was in high school, but it was hardly what he wanted to do with his life. Billy Joel might have gone on from there to become a massive star, but he was the exception, rather than the rule. What he needed, he knew, was a career with real prospects, and he could keep playing his music on the side, for fun. Music was the dream that filled his heart, but his head told him to look elsewhere.

"In high school, I was always debating whether to go to college, or to follow my dream into entertainment, or whether to go to the Air Force and become a pilot."

Flying fascinated him, and he could easily imagine himself training, then sitting in an F-114. So it was no surprise that one of his favorite movies was *Top Gun*, which had helped make a superstar out of Tom Cruise.

Of course, by now Kevin was becoming a megahunk himself. He'd grown to the same height as his father, six feet one, and had fleshed out to 175 pounds. And with his black hair and flashing green eyes, he was the type of guy all the girls wanted. But there was one that he had his eye on.

In his senior year of high school, Kev began dating a girl called Beth. Though he'd seen a lot of girls, this was different, and it quickly became more serious. For the first time, Kevin was in love.

It was a real relationship that went beyond just dating. By the end of his senior year, Kev and Beth were engaged, and even talking about getting married in time.

There were more immediate problems he had to face, however, namely what to do with his life. He felt split in two directions, and went to his father for advice.

"I talked to him about what I wanted to do with my life," Kevin remembers. "I was gonna join the Air Force when I left high school. That was the logical thing to do, my brain told me to do that, whereas my heart told me to pursue my music, and my dad agreed. He told me to do whatever I wanted."

And so it was decided. Well, almost. Kevin went so far as to talk to an Air Force recruiter. At the same time he was trying to put a band together. He asked the serviceman "if I could get a little more time to see how the band was going to work out, and he said, 'No, you have to go now or you don't go at all.'" That was all Kevin needed to hear. He walked. Ironically, within just a few weeks, the band broke up. There was nothing else around Lexington that would further his career. The main options seemed like New York or Los Angeles, and Kevin already knew how many musicians moved there. Besides, he wasn't interested in playing rock 'n' roll. He loved R&B, and really wanted, eventually, to be singing that. What he needed was a job that would pay him to sing. Theater was out—he could act, but it wasn't what he was looking for—musical roles were few and far between, and although he liked drama, he wasn't dedicated to it.

Finally, an idea came to him. Disney World.

The Richardsons had been there before, when they'd vacationed in Florida, and Kevin, Tim, and Jerald, Jr. had all loved it. For Kevin it wasn't just the rides, but the entertainment. The people who worked in shows there were being paid to sing. And almost next door was Universal Studios, with a lot more opportunities for a young singer. And it was warm.

It seemed perfect.

Leaving home for the first time was difficult for Kevin. The family was close, and it meant parting from Beth, too. But if he was going to get ahead, Kevin had to give it a shot.

He wasn't going alone. Trey, his best friend from high school was coming with him, looking for adventure and fun, a chance to make some money, and also enjoy the freedom of being out on his own.

After eighteen years in Lexington, Orlando seemed like a fresh new world. Outside the city there were still orange groves, with their leaves and bright fruit. The city was inland, almost fifty miles from the water, but that didn't bother Kevin; if he really wanted, he could still drive to the beach in an hour.

As it was, there was plenty to occupy him. Disney World, with the sparkling dome of EPCOT Center, seemed just as magical as it had when he was younger. And it seemed even better when he got a job there. It almost seemed like a dream, reporting for work there every day, knowing he was going to be paid for dressing up, entertaining, even if he was just starting out as a guide.

When he wasn't earning his paycheck, Kevin would keep in shape by playing basketball or working out with weights, or he'd just sit in his apartment and play music.

What he was doing was satisfying for now, but he had bigger dreams for the future.

Being at Disney was a good apprenticeship, however. He learned about staging and dancing, and even more about singing for people.

Everything was looking good. He was enjoying life—except for one aspect—his romance with Beth. A long-distance relationship is difficult enough under the best of circumstances. But at eighteen, it was nearly impossible. By that time, Kevin remembers, "We had dated for a year, and I thought that we were right for each other, but we found out that we didn't really know each other at all. I was too young and I wasn't ready."

The engagement was over, Kevin was alone again, heartbroken. In the fall of 1990 the rest of his family came down to visit, partly for a vacation, but more to see how the youngest Richardson was getting along. They stayed for a week, everyone having a great time, before going home, leaving Kev with some great memories.

But no sooner were his parents back in Lexington than the worst thing in the world happened—his father was diagnosed with colon cancer.

If treated quickly, the survival rate from colon cancer is good. Jerald, Sr. and Anne, not wanting to worry their boys unduly, didn't tell their sons immediately. Instead Jerald, Sr. went straight into hospital to have his tumor removed. At first it seemed as if he was going to be fine.

Tests were carried out, and it was discovered that the cancer the doctors believed they'd removed had already spread through Jerald, Sr.'s body.

Now they couldn't avoid telling the boys.

"When I was told, I was devastated," Kevin says. "I moved back home to Kentucky to be with him. He lived for ten months after his diagnosis."

Tim had stayed in Lexington, but Jerald, Jr., who was making his living as a model in Dallas, also moved home. The whole family rallied around, but there was little they could do except offer support and watch their father die.

After a spell in the hospital, Jerald, Sr. was allowed home, but returning regularly for chemotherapy.

"Then the chemotherapy caused clots in his blood," Kevin recalls. "He had a stroke, which affected his heart, so they put him back into the hospital. The doctors thought it was over, but he lived through that, too."

Kevin never believed that his father would die. Things like that just didn't happen.

Through it all Anne had to be strong for her sons. They were all grown, but even so they weren't ready for this. Finally, on August 26, 1991, Jerald Wayne Richardson passed away, at the age of forty-nine. At first, Kevin admits, "I felt very angry at God. I doubted Him." Though he may not have yet completely come to terms with his anger, he has realized that his family isn't alone in its sorrow. With cancer and AIDS, many families have been robbed of their loved ones before their time. That was a consolation of sorts, but only of sorts. Whenenver Christmas comes around, Kevin misses his father most of all.

". . . [I]t brings back memories of out times with him when I was growing up."

In his acknowledgments on *Backstreet Boys*, Kevin dedicated the album to his father's memory, and when the band collected their Select MTV Award in 1996, Brian remembered his uncle, saying, "To our family and friends, whether you're watching at home or above, thank you. . . ." Kevin was too emotional to say it himself. But, he says, "if I have the chance again, I'll mention him. I love my father and I want him to be remembered."

Kevin was still grieving, but life had to go on. He had to be as strong as his mother and move ahead with his own life—and that life was in Florida. In the fall of 1991 he moved back and returned to work at Disney, more determined than ever to make something of himself, something that would do justice to his father.

A year later he was still at Disney. After going back, he was a Teenage Mutant Ninja Turtle for a while, before moving on to performing in the Aladdin stage show. But he was also going out on other auditions, looking to spread his wings a bit. It had been twelve months of slowly healing, coming to terms with what had happened.

At some of the auditions, there were faces he'd see often, including three guys who seemed to be friends, although they were an odd group, ranging from around his age to one who looked like a kid of maybe twelve. They'd sing and laugh together, and Kevin would hear their harmonies on songs by Shai and Boyz II Men and think that perhaps he could fit in there. But he didn't try to introduce himself. One of the auditions took him to Lou Pearlman's office, where a friend of Kevin's worked. Lou had run an ad, looking for singing talent. It was obvious that Kevin could sing so well and had plenty of other talents. What he needed was to hook up with some other guys who could sing. Kevin's friend told him about these three guys, and suggested he hook up with them. . . .

These days, of course, Kevin is the big brother of the Boys, although he's not even a year older than Howie-D. He's still the quiet, slightly reserved one who hangs back a little bit. It's that childhood shyness that's come back a little in the wake of his father's death. And occasionally it can cause a bit of confusion.

"Sometimes when people meet me, they may think I'm stuck on myself," he explains. "I think I give people a bad first impression. They may interpret my shyness as being snobby or being high and mighty. That's the last thing I want people to think of me, so it concerns me.''

But once you get to know him a little, and he relaxes, Kevin becomes the perfect Southern gentleman, charming, talkative, and funny.

With a favorite color of blue—being from the Bluegrass State, home of the Kentucky Wildcats who wear blue, how could it be anything else?—he's very single, and hasn't had any real serious relationships since Beth, which suits him fine for right now. Not that he hasn't had girlfriends, but romance hasn't figured in the picture.

''I think romance is a total waste of time,'' he says. ''Of course, a candlelit dinner is nice, but it's got nothing to do with romance.''

He's just being honest—and honesty is definitely one of his traits, something he looks for in any potential girlfriend. On top of that, ''[s]he's got to be intelligent and confident about what she's saying. It's important that we can talk about everything.'' He loves a beautiful smile and a classy dresser—and classy *doesn't* mean short skirts, but something with real style and classic sex appeal.

If you're ever lucky enough to go out with Kevin (whose secret nicknames, by the way, are Boo and Pumpkin), you'd better expect a *lot* of attention. Not from other BSB fans, but from the hunk himself. When he's dating someone, ''I like to be with her all the time.'' But if he seems a little tongue-tied, that's just his shyness coming out again, being afraid he might end up saying the wrong thing. He's a great believer in good manners, having them himself and expecting them in return.

''If a girl's too loud and tries to get too much attention it kind of puts me off a little bit,'' he admits. ''And if they don't have very good manners, or if I hear them swearing, then that turns me off, too.''

When the Boys go on the road—and they *always*

seem to be on tour these days—Kevin makes sure he has his keyboard with him to help pass the long hours in hotel rooms and on buses traveling between shows. And finally he's begun playing onstage, letting the fans hear the result of all those years of practice. And it's something he's happy to do, to give his all for the people who come out to see them.

"I just kind of step back and take in everything around me. I see all the people smiling and laughing and crying and having a good time. What I do is for them, and it's something positive."

When he's abroad, he loves to sample the local foods, and he loves Mexican and Chinese, but, he says, "After a while I miss good American food."

These days, Kev shares an apartment in Orlando with Howie and Brian, not that he has much chance to be there any more. He doesn't need a big, expensive house in his life, or a flashy car—even after the Boys started making it big he drove a Honda Accord, finally trading it in on his dream car, a black Toyota 4Runner. But when he does get some time to relax in his room—which is decorated in black and white, and very sparsely furnished, he just likes to chill.

"I go see a movie or rent a video and stay at home. Sometimes I'll watch TV and play my keyboard."

He likes to wear silver rings on his fingers—and he'll move them from finger to finger—and a silver and leather bracelet on his right wrist. While he usually wears earrings, on the video of "Anywhere For You" he removed them.

While he's only ten months older than Howie, there's a real maturity about Kevin that makes him the natual leader of the Boys. And the rest accept that as a natural thing, says Howie.

"He's mature, responsible, professional, and knows what he wants . . . He's the authoritative one. You need someone like that, who has the leadership qualities to get the guys together.''

If Kevin has one fault (and it's hard to believe), it's that he's a perfectionist, which means he ends up demanding too much of others—and even more of himself.

''He's got a lot of positive aspects,'' says Brian, ''but he lets his perfectionist side get in the way sometimes because he wants things to be too perfect. He knows he has to lighten up . . .''

But Kevin, like all the others, is completely focused on the band. Sure, there's plenty of time for fun; still, he points out, ''Backstreet Boys is our life right now. We're pretty much eating, sleeping, and living it.''

And, really, he wouldn't have it any other way. He set out for Florida with a dream, and found the gold at the end of the rainbow. He's had a big loss along the way, one he'll never completely get over, but it's made him into a stronger person, one who'll do what he believes is right.

Kevin is the rock on which the Backstreet Boys are built. He's there for the other guys if they need him, whether it's on the road or at home. And he knows his family—and his fans—are going to be there for him. The perfect moment for him is to be onstage, looking out into the audience, and see them singing along with the lyrics.

''When you see someone singing your song, it's pretty wild. It can almost make you want to cry.''

♪ HOWIE ♪

America's history has been as a melting pot of races and colors. It's the new world, with plenty of opportunities for those who can come and take them. But few places have become the kind of melting pot that Florida is. Not only do the warm weather, beaches, and blue ocean attract tourists from all over the world, but the weather brings people to live there. Hot summers, warm winters, plenty to do, it's hardly surprising it's become a mecca.

And not just for snowbirds and retirees escaping the winter blasts of the North. For Latinos, the Florida climate isn't just a reminder of home, but as close as they can get, physically, while staying on the American mainland.

Florida was where Hoke Dorough, whose family had originated in Ireland, met Paula, his wife to be, during the 1950s. Paula's family origins included Puerto Rican ancestry. Back then Florida was still mostly rural. Even the big cities felt like small towns, before money moved in and began developing the land. After they married, the couple settled in Orlando, where Hoke worked, and began raising a family. First came Angie, born in 1960, then Caroline, two years later, Pollyanna in 1964, and John, the year after her.

With four children, it seemed as if things were complete, and Hoke and Paula settled into a routine with

their kids. Then, early in 1973, Paula had a surprise—
she discovered that she was going to have another baby!

By the time Howard Dwayne Dorough was born, on
August 22, 1973, Angie was already thirteen, and even
John, whom they'd always thought of as the youngest,
was eight. So that meant there was quite a gap between
Howie and his siblings; he was quite definitely the baby
of the family.

With so much life and activity going on around him,
it didn't take a lot to coax him out of his shell. Pollyanna
had shown an early inclination to performing, becoming
involved in musicals and plays at school and in local
community theater, but she was the only one with any
real dramatic or musical inclination in the family.

That made it particularly surprising when, one day,
Howie and his parents were visiting his grandmother,
and the three-year-old jumped on her bed and began
singing "Baby Face"! It was a song Paula had sung with
him, but she had no idea he remembered the words or
the tune, let alone that he had it in him to be such a
ham!

With one daughter already involved in music and
drama, Hoke and Paula did wonder if Howie might follow after her, but for the moment they decided not to
encourage it. Instead, they decided, if it was in him, it
would come out of its own accord. Better to let him have
a normal childhood than try to push him in any direction.

To the family, he was "Little Howie," being so much
younger than the others. And while he was a very good
kid—hardly needing any discipline, thinking about others—Paula notes, "He always needed to be busy doing
something; anything but sit around." Little Howie
couldn't bear to be bored. There always had to be some
activity going on with him. Once he learned to ride a
bicycle, that took some of his energy, and his favorite
toy became, "My Batman motorcycle," he remembers,
"it was one you could actually ride. I rode the heck out

of that, I thought I was Robin. I could do wheelies on it, but I kept busting my butt.''

When he wasn't out riding on the sidewalks around the Dorough house, Howie was singing; he loved it. In church, he became a young member of the choir. By the time he was seven, Pollyanna had been doing theater for a long time and decided that, since her little brother seemed to be a natural performer, he really ought to get involved, too, and be a show-off on the stage.

''She just tagged me along with her to all the musicals and plays she was in,'' Howie explains. ''The very first play I did was 'The Wizard of Oz.' I was a munchkin. She was Glenda, the Good Witch.''

It was almost the last play he did, as well. They needed munchkins, and Little Howie was the perfect size. But they didn't have a costume small enough to fit him. So when the rest of the Doroughs went to watch the first performance, they found Howie in pants that were way too big for him.

''When he danced they always fell down, and he constantly had to grab them to keep them up!'' Paula Dorough remembers with a laugh.

For a boy of seven to keep losing his pants onstage could easily have meant the end of a career in show business. Embarrassment at that age isn't easily forgotten—or lived down, for that matter, particularly when you're the youngest in a family, no matter how close-knit they may be.

But it seemed to have the opposite effect on Howie. It was as if he discovered very early what he wanted to do with his life. Tagging along with Pollyanna wasn't a chore, it was a pleasure, and once the local casting directors got to know Howie, and saw his talent, he became something of a fixture on the local musical theater scene, something totally different to the school plays he was always taking part in.

But it wasn't just theater and musicals that Howie

enjoyed. Pop music was on the radio, and MTV had just started, so there was plenty going on—most particularly Michael Jackson.

"Michael had a big influence on my life, in terms of inspiring me to sing," Howie admits. "He's a great artist. He's incredibly talented." And, more than anything, it was *Thriller*, which came out at the end of 1982, when Howie was an impressionable nine years old, spawning hit singles like "Beat It" and "Billie Jean," that really fired his interest. For a while, Michael was *it*. "... I had the album, I had Michael Jackson's glove, and I even had the Thriller skateboard."

But there didn't seem to be too many chances for a nine-year-old in Orlando to become the next Michael Jackson. Still, there were plenty of dance moves to copy and work out from the videos, including the famous Moonwalk that Jackson had begun.

And there was the joy of musical theater. Having put his toe into the water, Howie simply dived into it. No longer was he thought of as Pollyanna's little brother, but someone in his own right. By the time he was twelve, he was a veteran of the local theater circuit, having appeared in a staggering twenty-seven productions!

He'd received a real grounding in performance, having been in "The Sound of Music," "Camelot," "Showboat," and many others. If there was a big musical, Howie knew about it, and the chances were he knew at least half the score.

It was a strong start, but he realized that if he was going to take it further, and maybe pursue a career doing this, or—as he secretly dreamed—working more in pop music, he needed real, professional training.

Hoke and Paula weren't about to argue. Howie had such ability and aptitude—and it hadn't interfered with this schoolwork—that they were happy to encourage him in something that obviously made him so happy.

So, when he was twelve, Howie Dorough began lessons in singing and dancing. He thought that his experience meant he already knew a lot, but what he quickly discovered was that he still had an awful lot to learn!

There weren't too many singing coaches in the Orlando area, so they were all busy. Howie stayed with his coach for a few years, then moved on. But he'd meet him again later, at a talent show, where the coach had come as support for one of his newer pupils, a boy named Alexander, or AJ, whom he introduced to Howie. That meeting would be the very first link in the chain that would lead to the Backstreet Boys.

But there was a long way to go before that. Howie knew *what* he wanted to do—to sing and dance, act, and entertain—but he didn't know how to go about it.

One thing that really helped was when the cable television network Nickelodeon opened its studios—in Orlando! It provided an opportunity for Howie and a lot of other kids to strut their stuff and maybe end up on television. Like so many more, he'd go down and audition for every show they were casting, and his break looked as though it was finally going to turn when he ended up in the pilot of a series called *Welcome Freshman,* playing exactly what he was, a high school student.

Although the filming went well, Nickelodeon decided to pass on the idea of the series, feeling it just didn't have what they were looking for, and Howie was back to square one in his career.

In his own life, though, things were moving along. Being good-looking, he'd never been short of girlfriends, and had his first kiss when he was twelve years old, at a party.

"We were playing spin the bottle," he remembers, "and I got my first three kisses off the three best-looking girls in the school. It was the best party I've ever been to!"

His first real date had to wait a couple of years, though.

"It was when I was fourteen and I was in this play with a girl who was a year older than me," he remembers. "Her mother came and picked both of us up 'cause I didn't want to come pick her up on my bicycle ... I wanted to smell good so I splashed on as much cologne as I could!"

He was also beginning to discover his Latin heritage. Although there was a little Spanish spoken in the Dorough household, Howie hadn't bothered with it until until he entered high school, where he began learning the language properly. It was a part of him, and he quickly realized just how much it really was.

"... [A]s I got older, through high school," he explains, "it was something I wanted to incorporate."

He began listening to the Spanish language records that were available all over Florida, and began to see just how popular performers like Selena, Gloria Estefan, and, in particular, Jon Secada, were. Becoming bilingual was important to him (and it's something he's passed on to the rest of the Boys—Howie was the one who suggested they record two of their songs, "Anywhere For You," and "I'll Never Break Your Heart" in Spanish), and it remains so. He'd still like to record and perform with Secada.

The series with Nickelodeon might not have happened, but that was hardly the end of the road for Howie. There were plenty of other opportunities around, and once the new Disney MGM and Universal studios were up and running in the area, the potential for work really increased. In 1988, at the age of fifteen, Howie found himself on a movie set for the first time, with a part in *Parenthood,* the comedy directed by Ron Howard and starring Steve Martin, with a young Keanu Reeves also showing up in the cast list. Howie only had a bit part—

blink and you'd miss him—but it was a start, another credit to add to the resume that was rapidly getting very long indeed!

He thought it would lead to more work, but it didn't, at least not immediately. He was going out on auditions, still acting in local theater, taking singing and dancing lessons, and going through his apprenticeship as a performer. There was one bright spot, making a commercial for Disneyworld, but the offers still weren't coming in thick and fast.

In his last year of high school he met a girl, Jennifer, and they started dating regularly. On a school trip to New York, he took the opportunity to tell the world just how he felt about her at the Statue of Liberty.

"I was going up a spiral staircase that led to the top and I saw everybody else's name and thought, 'What the heck?' "

And she, too, had strong feelings for him. On his eighteenth birthday, "she asked her parents if she could have the house to herself, and invited all my friends round for a surprise party! That was really romantic!"

The romance wasn't all on her side, though. During the two years they were together, "I once cooked dinner for her—it was grilled steaks and candles and everything. Then afterwards we drove to the airport, because there's this strip in Orlando where you can sit, look at the stars and watch the planes going over."

He even sang her a song he'd written for her—one of the few songs he's penned—so far.

"I was walking along the beach with [her] when I started singing the song I'd written for her. It's always very heartwarming when that happens."

Unfortunately, it all came to an end, as did another relationship Howie had afterward, leaving Howie with a broken heart twice!

"Neither of them could deal with my career. I respect them for being honest, but it still really hurt."

After graduating high school, Howie was wondering what he was going to do with his life. In his heart, he knew what he wanted, but his parents urged him to go to college, and get a solid education before he really tried to make a living from his art. And he agreed. There was nothing else going on, and college seemed useful, so he enrolled at community college, taking courses, but still making sure he had enough time to attend all the auditions in the area.

In 1992 he struck lucky again, getting a small role in a film aimed at kids, *Cop and a Half,* with a Florida legend among its stars—Burt Reynolds. Again, Howie didn't have much of a part, but it was better than nothing. And maybe, he thought, his luck would begin to finally turn after this.

He knew auditions were part of the whole game, but that didn't make them any less boring: sitting around for hours, waiting for maybe five minutes on a stage to show what you could do. Over and over, it seemed like he'd see the same faces waiting, hoping just like him for a big break. One face he seemed to see a lot was familiar, and when they started talking, he knew where he'd seen the guy before—it was AJ, who'd gone to the same singing teacher as Howie. They began discussing music and discovered that they both loved Prince and all manner of R&B. It wasn't long before they started singing together and realizing that their voices worked well in harmony, with Howie having a falsetto range that would allow him to easily reach the high notes. AJ had another friend, a young kid who was also making it to the auditions, who could really sing, too, and soon they were making music together, and understanding that they had something going on. . . .

These days Howie, or Howie-D as people call him (or Sweet D, because he really is so sweet), doesn't have too much time for anything but BSB. But that doesn't mean that all work and no play makes Howie a dull Boy! Quite the opposite; there's still plenty of time to have fun. Where Backstreet are touring, the way they always are, he's the one who's out with Kevin after shows, going to the hippest clubs and checking out new dance moves the Boys can use in their act. Clubbing is something he just *loves* to do And he'll be the one with the camcorder on the bus or when the guys get a chance to do a little sightseeing, making tape after tape to send to his family.

Howie may be a huge international star these days, but his family is still the most important thing to him. They've stayed close-knit, and, in fact, they're his relaxation.

"I chill out by calling my family and having a chat with them," he explains. ". . . Calling my family forces me to sit down and be calm for a bit—otherwise, if I'm really stressed, I'll just crash out."

One thing that hasn't changed from when he was a little kid is that Howie stills gets bored easily. He *needs* to be doing things.

"The only sports I enjoy are racquetball and water-skiing. I'm a very active person so for me to sit down and watch TV or something feels like a total waste of time when there are a million and one other things I could be doing."

You're likely to find Howie wearing a vest, his favorite item of clothing.

"I've got about forty vests at home," he says, "from dressy, to wild, to old-fashioned ones. My favorite is a red and mustard one."

Trying to get him to pack them for another BSB trip isn't that easy, though. He's a neat freak, who keeps his room in the apartment he shares with Kev and Brian spotless. But he also likes to be precise about packing, making sure everything fits just perfectly, and nothing's going to get too creased. All too often, though, it doesn't matter. Of all the Boys, Howie's the one whose luggage seems to end up far away from the country it was headed for; it's just his luck.

But when the occasional argument does flare in the band—and hey, they *are* just human, after all—it's Howie who's always the peacemaker.

"Howie's Mr. Mediator," says AJ. He's the one who makes sure that the peace is kept. But tempers never last for long, anyway. "Like brothers [we] may argue," AJ continues, "but the really cool part is that as soon as we walk off that bus it's just like walking into character. We always make up. There's never any twenty-four-hour 'I hate you' kind of thing. And Howie's like, 'C'mon guys, let's be serious. Let's be focused.' "

He has his rituals. Before every show he drinks hot tea with lemon and honey to help his voice through the evening. And every night, without fail, he does his sit-ups to keep his stomach muscles firm—not that he needs it, the way he moves onstage!

But one Howie secret is that he sometimes snores, according to Nick, who used to be his roommate on the road. "I stuck a bit of Kit Kat in his mouth once," Nick recalls of a joke he played on his crashed bud, "and he tried to take a bite out of it in his sleep!"

The Latin Lover doesn't have too much time to spend with the ladies these days (although there are plenty who'd like to spend a lot of time with him), but that doesn't mean he doesn't have his fixed idea of his dream girls.

He has a very definite fixation on Cindy Crawford. In London the Boys had passes to a very exclusive club and were hanging there when Cindy walked in. Howie couldn't even put the words together to speak to her. That's not too surprising, since he says, "A lot of people think I'm shy. But once they get to know me, they realize I'm not shy at all."

One thing Howie doesn't really go by in the real world

is looks (okay, Cindy is an exception). For him the personality is much more important, someone who's supportive of what he does, and what he's going to be doing for a long time to come. She'd better also like to have fun—and dancing is a good place to start.

"The dance floor—dancing's a great way to meet people!"

Best of all, he likes to hug and hold. "I think it's because I grew up in a big family," he explains. "Even now, I grab my mom and give her big kisses on the cheeks. When I'm with a girl, I love her to give me hugs—it touches my heart. I could use a hug every day." Along with the hugs, he also likes to talk a lot, and also a lot of surprises, like whisking a girl away for a weekend with hardly any notice, about as good a reason as any to keep a bag packed and ready, just in case.

One thing he does look forward to, eventually, is starting a family of his own.

"I can't say how long from now, I don't know. First I have to find the girl of my dreams. But someday, for sure, I'll start a family."

Like Kevin, he doesn't need an expensive house or car to show his status. He still sometimes goes out on his own in Orlando, and manages to be unrecognized with a baseball cap pulled low over his eyes. For a long time he drove a Mazda 626, until the Boys went car shopping and he put in his order for a 1997 Corvette. He has two of his bandmates for his roomies, although his neatness against Brian's legendary messes can't be too easy to deal with.

Although he doesn't play onstage, Howie has mastered the guitar—it's right there on the "Quit Playing Games (With My Heart)" video, so it might not be too long before he's joining Kevin's keyboards, Nicks' drumming, and AJ's bass onstage.

One thing Howie will find onstage is Gummi Bears, according to AJ.

"Howie mentioned in one interview, way back," he explains, "that he liked Gummi Bears . . . Every night on stage, boxes of Gummi Bears!"

Like all the others, the Boys are his main focus for now. The rest of the world is crazy for them, but America is just beginning to catch up, and that's where they really want to succeed. Being big at home, up there with the people they modeled themselves on, like Boyz II Men, is important to Howie. And for now he's loving the way the fans in America have taken them all into their hearts.

"It's all new to us, we're enjoying it, you know, every minute of it!" he says.

And like Kevin, AJ, Brian, and Nick, Howie is very grounded. All the adulation hasn't gone to his head. His family makes sure of that! They remain his center, so that even when the girls are screaming, his head won't swell. He's worked hard, for many years, to get where he is today. When he first took the stage as a munchkin all that time ago, he couldn't have predicted that now he'd be getting mobbed. But this was what he was working toward all the time, and it's finally happened. Persevering at things really does pay off!

♪ BRIAN ♪

Catch them on their own, and each of the Boys is a little shy. They all agree, though, that Brian is the one who's most reserved.

In some ways he's even more serious than Kevin, although he can also be the funniest of the group. Brian Thomas Littrell was born on February 20, 1975, in Lexington, Kentucky. His parents, Jackie and Harold—Harold is the brother of Kevin's mom, Anne—already had a boy, Harold Baker Littrell III, who was three, the same age as Kevin, in fact.

From a very early age, Brian was interested in music, and as a toddler he began singing almost as soon as he could speak. Jackie was very involved with her church, and she took the boys with her every Sunday. Soon Brian knew the hymns, and once he was old enough, joined the choir, where he quickly became one of the stars.

"I never dreamed of being a big star or anything," he says quietly. "I grew up in a big Baptist church and ever since I could walk I was singing."

When he was five, however, Brian's life, and that of his family, changed. He began to get sick, and the doctors rushed him to hospital with a heart infection that could have been fatal. For a while he was in very serious condition, until the treatment began to work. Even then, his recuperation took a long time, and that meant Jackie had to be there every day to see her son.

"When I was dealing with the stuff in the hospital we were all surviving off my dad's income."

That made for a financial strain on the family, since Jackie had always worked, and they relied on her earnings to supplement Harold's. But once Brian was fully recovered—which took several months—she returned to work.

One thing that sustained the Littrells through that time was their faith, and it was—and remains—an important rock to Brian.

"I'm not real religious," he admits, "but my family brought me up with a religious background. I try to stay somewhat focused on that and do my own thing."

That thing, more and more, became singing at church. He became a soloist in the choir, often performing in other churches, revivals, tent mettings, anywhere he was asked to open his mouth. In school, though, he tended to keep quiet about it, partly because he didn't want to sound vain, and also because no one seemed to care about church singing.

But there was also another side to Brian. He was the regular kid who loved basketball (and his performances on the court, shooting hoops would lead to his nickname, B-Rok), and the music on the radio. His favorite singer was, and still is, Luther Vandross.

He took part in the usual grade school plays—like everyone else, he didn't really have a choice—but theater and acting didn't really interest him too much then. Singing was his life.

When his voice broke, it sounded even better than it had before, sweeter and more mature. But one thing that never occurred to him was to take voice lessons. Singing was just something he *did*; the idea of possibly making a living from it never occurred to him.

Harold and Jackie raised their boys right. To get their

allowances they had to do their chores—Brian's were to take out the trash and run the dishwasher. They made sure their sons had everything they needed, but when it came to things they might want, both Harold III and Brian had to demonstrate a sense of responsibility about money.

Brian first learned that lesson when he was sixteen. His brother already had a car—he was working, and could afford one—and Brian wanted one, too, to be able to get around, and take out his dates. Jackie, however, said, "You're not getting a car until you get a job, save some money, put a nice down payment on it and pay it off!" No argument, no fuss; that was simply the way it was going to be!

Brian knew what he had to do. He found himself a job, first helping out at his church and organizing the sanctuary for weddings. He wasn't about to make his fortune—or even enough for a used car—doing that, so he began working part-time at Long John Silver's, a fast-food fish and chip chain, based in Kentucky. It wasn't easy work, always hot and sweaty with the deep-fat fryers behind him and having to be pleasant to all the customers, but Brian did it after school and on weekends.

Juggling all the things he had to do was particularly difficult. He had to keep up his grades, make sure his homework was done, fulfill all his singing obligations with the church, and still find time to have a little fun with his girlfriends—and Brian, being very cute, had lots of them!

Over the course of eighteen months, he managed to prove to his parents that he really was responsible and trustworthy, and they helped him buy a car, which gave him the freedom he was looking for as a teenager.

Brian also liked to sing with Kevin. His older brother played the drums a little but didn't have much of a voice. It was his cousin who was the other singer in the family. As they were all close, they'd see each other often and harmonize on hits, with Brian usually taking the lead—his voice was just naturally so good, powerful, and emotive. Still, though, Brian didn't think of it as a career—he thought he'd probably end up as a physical education teacher after college. He loved sports, and was still crazy about basketball, particularly the Kentucky Wildcats, and could relax by shooting baskets on the hoop his dad had put up above the garage door or getting on a court with some of his friends and playing a game.

All through high school, he was a great romantic. With one girl he really liked, he discovered the combination to her locker, and put a dozen red roses inside.

"She started crying when she saw them," he recalls.

Everything changed, though, during his junior year of high school. Kevin was in Florida, working at Disneyworld, so Brian really didn't have anyone around to sing with.

On top of that, he felt like his world had just collapsed, since he'd been dumped by Shannon, a girl he'd liked for two years, after they'd gone out for three months and three days. Brian had met her back in the ninth grade and quickly became smitten. He'd even started going to her church and taking part in the youth group she attended! This was true love! But for two years she hardly seemed to notice he existed.

But what Brian had been attracted to was a pretty face. All his friends had told him to watch out, but he didn't want to believe it—until he got to know her properly. He came to believe that she could be mean under the beauty, and that just turned Brian off her.

"I finally got my chance and it just didn't turn out," he recalls. "When I look back on it, it was just an experience . . ."

But it wasn't as huge an experience as the one he'd go through the next semester. All through school, no one had paid much attention to his singing, although they loved his voice at church. He was part of the chorus, and even took chorus class, but he was just one of the group . . . until he got onstage for the talent show.

He'd already agreed to perform a song with a girl from the chorus, a spiritual called "Another Time, Another Place." It was in front of the *whole* school, every student crammed into the auditorium to listen. Brian was dressed for the occasion in a suit and tie, a little nervous at performing in front of all these people who knew him. But singing was second nature to him now.

Brian's partner started off, singing the first line, then Brian entered. Before he'd even sung a whole line, all the girls in the audience were screaming. At first, blinded by all the spotlights, he wondered what was going on, until he realized they were screaming for *him*!

After three words he couldn't even hear himself for the rest of the song, the noise was so loud. He was just amazed at the reaction; all of a sudden Brian Littrell was a *star*!

That moment showed him "that if I could pull off something like that with my peers, then there definitely had to be people out in the world who would like it as well."

Inevitably, news about Brian's triumph reached Kevin in Florida through family phone calls. So a year later, when BSB were looking for that elusive fifth member, he remembered the stir Brian's singing had caused at school. That was all the others needed to know.

But Brian was actually the last person to hear that he was being auditioned for the Boys. On April 6, 1993, he was pulled from U.S. history class, his last period of the day, to take a mysterious phone call. It was Kevin, in Orlando, asking if he could fly down the following day and see if he fitted in with the other guys.

To say B-Rok was excited on his way home from school was putting it mildly. He rushed in the door and said, "Mom, I gotta tell you, I gotta tell you!"

She already knew. Kevin, being the good nephew, had

talked to Jackie and Harold before he placed the called to Brian. Naturally, his mom was concerned about his education. Brian only had two months to go before graduation, and she didn't want him blowing that off.

So that evening, she spent a long time talking to Denise, AJ's mother, and learning about the tutoring system. Both AJ and Nick were still in school, spending time with tutors every day, making sure they kept up on their studies. If everything went well at Brian's audition, he could study with them for his remaining two months.

When all that was setlled, Jackie called the Boys' managers, who told Brian, "You've got to get down here and audition. We've heard a lot of great things about you and you've got to give it a shot!"

That was all Brian needed. Jackie and Harold were convinced that it couldn't hurt, and a flight was booked for the next morning, although it was hardly worth Brian going to bed; he was way too excited to sleep.

At 6 A.M., April 7, he was on a plane leaving Louisville for Orlando. Kevin was waiting at the airport to meet him, in the kind of style he hadn't expected—there was a limo parked outside the terminal. These were his wildest dreams happening, and he was ready for them.

Then he met the other guys, they sang together, and that was all anyone needed to know. Brian was a Backstreet Boy, born for the job . . .

You'd better believe he loves being one of the guys, too.

"I wouldn't change a thing in my life," he says. "I thank God for everything."

He means that literally, too. Whenever the Boys go on tour, the one thing he makes sure he has in his carry-on is his book of spiritual lessons.

Success has meant a lot to him, not least the chance to give presents to his family. Older brother Howard received a new car to replace the one he had, and Brian gave Jackie a new piano to put in the house in Lexington.

Once he became one of the Boys, he instantly struck up a close friendship with Nick. The five-year age gap between them really didn't seem to matter; they just had so much in common. Both of them love basketball, and can also play Nintendo for hours at a time.

"The main thing I remember about Nick when I first met him," Brian recalls, "is how small he was. He was so energetic and full of life—I was like, '*Wow*!' I was totally bowled over, and then I heard his voice. Man, it was just so big for this little guy."

And Nick was equally impressed.

"It was weird considering I was so young. I just knew we'd get on—we had so much in common, and Brian was exactly the same then as he is now. We related so well!"

So well that they became best buds. Brian is Frick and Nick is Frack. Often they'll even room together if Nick's parents don't accompany him on the road.

In many ways, Brian has become Nick's older brother (and Nick's now like Brian's younger brother). Certainly Nick enjoys being with him. ". . . Brian is sooo cool. I can't think of one bad thing to say about him, he's so much fun to be around."

And, according to Nick, Brian has adjusted to fame very well; there's no danger of it going to his head.

"He's totally stayed the same," Nick says. "I don't think it's affected him at all."

About the only luxuries Brian's indulged in are his Jeep—the one with the 'B-ROK' license plate that he washes in the video (although he did buy himself a brand-new one, painted green)—and a gold necklace he had made in Sydney, Australia, that also spells out B-Rok. That's something he won't part with. One time, when the Boys were being mobbed by screaming fans, and some were trying to rip the necklace off, he hung onto it tightly, even though he ended up with scratches all over his neck.

Musically, even though he's been all over the world and heard a lot of great music, he still loves Boyz II Men and his favorite, Luther Vandross.

"I admire him as a singer because I saw him live in Orlando," he says. "I would give anything for a copy of that concert. It was just unbelievable. He just blew me away."

Even after the awards and the mega-hits, Brian is still really into the singing; it's what he loves. He believes we're all here for a reason: "Which for me is singing and being a ham on stage."

And he has the perfect job for it. Anyone who's seen the Boys knows that Brian sings a lot of the leads, something he's very proud of. And he realizes how lucky he is to be doing something he loves and getting paid for it. This is his dream job. "I never dreamed it would be worldwide," he admits. "It's still kind of a little hard to believe."

If you *have* seen the Boys, you'll know that Brian really is a ham and a comedian in front of an audience.

"Joke telling isn't one of my big things but I like to make people laugh by pulling funny faces or tripping and falling over. Sometimes I hurt myself!"

That funny side, he feels, is one facet of him. "But I have another side, and when I'm talking about my emotions or how I am on the inside, I like to get into more detail."

Mostly, though, it's the happy Brian who's in charge, although catch him first thing in the morning, if he's gotten up on the wrong side of the bed, and you're likely to find a grouch. Not on Sunday, though. If there's a chance, Brian will go to church to attend a service.

In many ways, he's the most traditional guy in the band, and, everyone says, the one who'll probably be the first married BSB.

All he needs first is a girlfriend. He takes the idea of love and romance very seriously. "I guess in that way, I am sort of old-fashioned," he admits, "and I'd have to say that honestly, I don't believe in having a sexual relationship outside of marriage." But those are the moral and religious views that were a part of his upbringing, and have stayed with him.

If he ever does get enough time to really catch his breath, and really enjoy a serious relationship, his ideal girl has long hair and blue eyes (his two big ideals are Pamela Lee and Sandra Bullock, but we're talking real life here). And pretty hands, which are especially important to him. She'd also have to share his sense of humor—which can be quite wicked at times—and his values. And be willing to put up with his mess—in the apartment, it's agreed that his room is always the untidy one. But the lucky girl who gets him might be able to cure Brian of his only real bad habit—biting his nails.

But if you do ever get the chance to be alone with him, one sure way to win him over is to run your fingers through his hair. "I like a girl to play with my hair— y'know, rough and tumble my head."

Of course, a time out to develop a love interest simply hasn't happened for any of the Boys in the last few years as they've built up their fan base around the world. But when they do get back to Orlando, and Brian can take a little time at the apartment he shares with Kevin and Howie, his way of chilling is to "lie on the couch and just watch TV—that's it!" On the road he never has that opportunity, so put him there, with a football or a basketball game playing, and maybe some macaroni and cheese cooking, and you've got yourself one very contented BSB. And when he's ready to go to sleep, in his room he has the "practically new" king-size waterbed that he picked up for just $50!

While Kevin and Howie are adventurous eaters, Brian definitely isn't. Instead of trying the local cuisine, he's more likely to head for the nearest McDonald's. "I'm more or less just a meat and potatoes kind of man," he explains. "We have such a tight schedule that you don't really want to get ill, so sticking to what you know might be boring, but at least you get to perform."

Brian's never going to lose the sense that it's all about the fans. The possession he prizes most came from a fan, a girl in Florida named Brittany, who, with her mom's help, sent the Boys a gift through the fan club—little tee shirts with the Boys' names airbrushed on them. "It was just so neat to know that they went to all that trouble for us, you know," he says.

What you see with Brian is exactly what you get. He feels that "it's important to me that fans know what sort of person I am and what I'm all about. It's not that I want them to follow me or do as I do, but I just hope I set a good example."

Most of the time you'll find Brian to be very light-hearted, laughing with the guys, cracking jokes, or just taking one of them on at hoops.

Sometime in the future, he'd like to have the chance to go to college and get that phys. ed. degree, and maybe help out in schools as a volunteer, to be involved with the kids there. More immediately, though, he'd love to be a VJ, or possibly get a role in a Jim Carrey movie. Although he's never really acted, it's something he'd like to try, and along with the others, there has been some talk of a BSB movie, to be based on the comic book major artist Nick has been working on. That, though, is for the future, and, Brian says, "I just don't know how long it's going to take."

Like all the others, the Boys are the real focus in his life at the moment. If he were to fall in love, and had to choose between romance and his career, it would be the girl who'd be left standing. ". . . I'd tell her, 'Time will tell, but I have things to do for myself right now.' "

But when the time and the person is right, he'll know

it, even if he does underplay the gifts he can bring to a relationship. "The main things I've got to offer are a little love, caring, understanding, and emotion," he says. Probably more than a little!

One thing Brian does realize is how lucky the Boys have been, and that, really, he's like the people in the audience. If it hadn't been for a series of circumstances (and a *great* voice), he'd be on the other side, still watching people perform himself.

"My logic is that my life is no different than anyone else's except for four or five feet, and that four or five feet is how tall the stage is. Because if you put anyone else on stage, the girls will scream. I'm just the lucky one who's having an opportunity like this. When I step off the stage, I'm like anyone else."

Well, maybe not *quite* like everyone else. There aren't many people who could have taken his lead on "Quit Playing Games (With My Heart) or "Don't Leave Me" (a track not included on their American album, for some reason), or could have his kind of presence on the stage. At five feet eight inches and 140 pounds, he's not the biggest of the Boys, not even close, but he definitely catches the eye and just oozes presence and charisma— no wonder so many people just love him.

Sometimes the fans do go a bit overboard. When the band first hit big in Europe, one of the fan magazines printed their real addresses in Florida, which led to Brian getting a surprise visit from two Swiss girls! Howie and Kevin were out, but Brian "drove my car into my apartment complex, and they knew my car because a picture of it had been in a magazine . . . These two girls were sitting right in front of my apartment with their pens and paper, and they jumped when they saw me."

Brian, of course, having been raised right, a charming Southern boy, was happy to give them autographs. When they'd come all that way to see him, how couldn't he!

But it was still a shock, in time that he'd thought was his own.

He's real—all the guys are real—but Frick is totally honest and upfront about himself. One thing Brian would never do, unless it was all in fun, of course, is play games. And he'd never cheat on a girl, either—all the Boys are agreed on that. Which is reassuring, but not too suprising to anyone who'd ever heard him talk or looked into those blue, blue eyes. If you ever get Brian, you've got him *all* the way. He's someone who believes in committment, in everything, including the band. "We're for real," he says. "What you see is what you get. We're five solo artists put together and we love to do what we do."

They're the perfect complement for each other, with Brian as both the humorous and spiritual sides of the group. If the band ever should break up, he's the one who'll probably begin singing gospel music, the church music he started out with. But that's not going to happen for a long time. For the moment he's enjoying it, taking everything as it comes, which, he insists, is all you can do.

"I think you have to take life day by day, and the more humor you find in everyday things then the happier you'll be. My grandmother on my dad's side is nearly eighty, but she looks like she's fifty, and acts like she's thirty."

For someone who says that "I just like to make people laugh," he makes everyone smile. But no one would think of laughing *at* Brian, not these days. Not when he's grown into a hunk with the voice of an angel. Even if he can spend a lot of time teasing the others.

"I take the mickey out of Howie 'cause he takes so long to do everything," Brian admits. "And Kevin 'cause he's the oldest. If he doesn't laugh with us we say, 'You're too much of an old man to understand our jokes.''

But that's okay, it's all good fun. And everyone knows he doesn't mean it. Brian is, at heart, one sweet, sweet guy.

♪ AJ ♪

Every band needs someone like AJ, who can get a little wild, who loves to party, who likes to get a little out on the edge at times. He's the one who pushes and tweaks the others a bit. Bone, as he is nicknamed, is the man. And even among five cool guys, AJ is definitely the coolest, always changing his hair color or length, and wearing his trademark sunglasses; he's really got it all goin' on.

Bob and Denise McLean loved Florida. It seemed like the perfect place to them, with its sun, palm trees, and ocean. On top of that, in the 1970s, there was plenty of opportunity down there for someone who wanted to get ahead. In particular they loved the city of West Palm Beach, about seventy-five miles north of Miami. It was still small enough to be sleepy, but it looked as though it might grow. And it did.

Once they were settled there, Denise discovered she was pregnant, and on January 9, 1978, Alexander James McLean came into the world. From the very first he was an active baby, and one who loved music, and one who'd carry the blanket he'd been given when he was born everywhere with him. Even before he was speaking, if there was music on television or the radio, he'd smile and bounce. And once he became a toddler, there was absolutely no stopping him.

"AJ was always full of energy," Denise says. "Everyone would say if we could bottle it, we'd make a fortune! He never stopped chattering or moving."

AJ would be the couple's only child. When he was four years old his parents divorced, as the marriage, sadly, hadn't worked out, and Denise would raise him on her own. She could see very early on that he loved to perform for people, to sing and dance, and that he had all the makings of an entertainer. But she didn't want to be a stage mom, pushing her son toward it all. She wanted him to have a really rounded childhood, to enjoy being a kid and not grow up too early.

What AJ's heart seemed set on, though, was completely different. He loved music and could spend hours singing along with the tapes on the boom box in his room. After he'd played Dopey in a grade school production of "Snow White and the Seven Dwarfs," he already knew what he wanted to do with his life. Being up on stage, making people laugh, singing for them, was just incredible.

Any form of entertaining seemed to attract him. When Denise bought him a puppet, he quickly learned the difficult skill of puppeteering, and would give shows for kids in the neighborhood. He still liked regular things, like shooting hoops or trips to the mall, but entertaining was pulling him every which way. So it was no surprise that he became involved in local theater, just as Howie had done in Orlando, winning roles in "The King and I," "Fiddler on the Roof," and even "The Nutcracker"!

By the time he was twelve, Denise knew that she couldn't deny AJ was a born entertainer, and the best thing she could do for him would be to help him along his way.

For someone like AJ, all the opportunities in Florida were in Orlando. Not only was that the home of Disneyworld, but also Universal Studios, and Nickelodeon, which was producing its own shows, and always needed talented child actors and singers.

To do things properly, though, AJ needed professional training—Denise was adamant that if AJ really was going to do this, he'd do it right, and learn from the pros. So once they were settled in their new home, she began to send him for dance lessons, where he mastered everything from tap to jazz, some ballet, and even learned how to breakdance. And there were also the voice lessons. AJ could sing, but there was still a lot he needed to learn, the best way to breathe, and how to use his voice properly as an instrument. That was how he ended up meeting Howie Dorough, who had shared the same teacher.

AJ might have been focused on his budding career, but that didn't mean there was no time for girls. He'd started young with them, although it hadn't been the most successful beginning. When he was four, he'd locked lips with a neighbor's daughter.

"I kissed her and she didn't like it, so she punched me in the stomach!" he laughs.

It seemed to put him off for a while, and he waited another eight years before enjoying his first serious kiss. And serious it was, with plenty of tongue, he admits, but not in the easiest position, "through a chain-link fence. I ended up with a big mark around my mouth from the . . . fence, and everybody was asking me what the mark around my mouth was!"

Actually, AJ didn't have much luck with the girls. Instead, a lot of bad things happened. When he was thirteen he was in love for the first time, and his girlfriend was killed in an automobile accident. The shock of that took a long time to wear off, but other relationships did eventually come. He met a girl who lived in Ohio, but who was on vacation in Florida. When she went home, AJ wanted to keep in touch with her, and he did—on the phone, which didn't please Denise when she received a long-distance bill for $200, since AJ had told that "he only made two or three calls for a few minutes apiece." By the time he was fifteen, just as the Boys were getting together, he fell in love with a girl called Melissa, who ended up dumping him in the coldest fashion.

"Everything was great until she moved to California with her family without letting me know, even though she knew months before that she'd be leaving."

And that came after AJ had done the most romantic thing of his life, to celebrate their first anniversary.

"There was a big box waiting for Melissa when she got home, and when she opened it I jumped out with a bouquet of roses . . . She was stunned!"

Of course, he wasn't the perfect boyfriend to Melissa, either. At an eighth grade dance, they were necking on the dance floor until she had to leave and go home. Then the romeo was on the prowl, kissing another girl, then another, until he'd kissed most of the girls there that night.

But he really did love Melissa, and frequently got into trouble over her at school, because she "went to class on the other side of the campus, so I'd walk her back after lunch and be late!"

Even once the band really started, when they were playing shopping malls, AJ had a girlfriend in Orlando, named Jennifer. This, he thought, was real love. He wrote poems to her, they talked about a future where they might end up getting married and being together forever. It all seemed perfect, until the day AJ caught her kissing another guy.

"When I asked her about it, she told me I was too serious and boring for her . . ." which is kind of hard to believe, given the crazy way AJ acts. But that *was* when everything about the Boys was new to him, and he had to take it all very seriously. Jennifer had been something of a BSB fan—she'd come to the early shows, and she knew what AJ was doing, but she didn't quite get it, and obviously didn't think he was worth waiting for. Big mistake.

That was the last serious relationship he's had; these days there's just no time.

Time was always at a premium for AJ, though. When he was younger there was homework, dance class, voice lessons, and he'd begun acting lessons as well, to become really well-rounded in his craft. Then there were all the auditions Denise had to drive him to.

Finally, it all seemed to be paying off. AJ landed a part of a short-lived Nickelodeon series called *Hi Honey, I'm Home*. It didn't last long, but people at the network were impressed by AJ's talents. So, too, were the people he auditioned for at the nearby Disney channel. It seemed like there was nothing he couldn't do very well—sing, dance, act, even manipulate puppets, a skill he'd begun in childhood and had kept up. Both Nickelodeon and Disney used him whenever they could, even though there were no featured roles. He was a talent to watch and nurture.

Still, he was able to feel that he was coming along. And he was still going to plenty of auditions. It was there he ran into Nick and also met Howie again. Since the three of them loved to sing so much, it was only natural that they'd end up all singing together. And so Backstreet was born. . . .

Once the band was going, Denise's biggest worry was about AJ's education. But their managers planned on taking care of that. It was obvious that both Nick and AJ—who was only fifteen at that point—would need a tutor, with lessons to be given every day, and plenty of study time in there with the traveling, rehearsing, and performing. It wouldn't be easy, and Denise and AJ knew that, but this was the kind of break that didn't happen every day. He *had* to take it.

These days, of course, he's very glad he did. AJ has

had a chance to see the world, to do things no twenty-year-old usually has the opportunity to do, as well as become a heartthrob. And it's given him a chance to express himself in song, although it's hard to believe such a deep voice could come out of someone who only stands five feet nine inches and weighs less than 130 pounds!

But he can also express himself in other, wilder ways, and he certainly does! If any one of the Boys loves to party, it's AJ. In 1996, he and Nick held a joint birthday party at their managers' house—AJ was turning eighteen, and Nick sixteen, and they both have birthdays in January—that lasted all night.

"There were about two hundred people there and we had a total blast," AJ recalls enthusiastically. "The guys threw me in the pool and I rubbed cake down Nick's shirt and in his hair. We spilled drinks all over the carpets and I didn't even have to tidy up afterwards! I fell asleep about six in the morning."

It's almost as if the energy he had when he was little has doubled. Like Howie, he loves to go out clubbing when he has the chance, and staying out until four or four-thirty if there's plenty going on, then trying to get up again an hour later is quite common for him when he's on the road.

He's even gone so far as to moon the guys in the band bus when they've been traveling on the freeways across Europe, although he'd never do it to anyone else, because, as he says, "I don't want strangers taking pictures to my mom!"

AJ's the BSB who's really into fashions. His hair has been plenty of different colors, ranging from platinum blond to almost black, and every shade in between. He's let it grow, and he's even had it cut really short (his hair is actually receding a little bit, so he likes to keep it really short).

He's also the most outgoing of all the guys. More than

anything, he loves to talk. "He's always on the phone to his family in Florida," Brian reveals. "I'd hate to see his phone bill. He'll chat to anyone and tell you stories all day long, whether they're true or not."

It's not just his family and friends that AJ likes talking to. Sometimes he'll even call up fans who've given him their phone numbers and just happily chat away for hours. So if you get a chance to be close to him, you might just want to have that number written on a piece of paper—you never know what might happen!

He readily admits he'd be lost without his phone, but talking is his form of relaxation and dealing with the stress of touring. When he gets a chance, he also likes to play pool, the only sport he's good at (although the other guys have got him into basketball), and listen to music or draw.

Musically his tastes are very similar to the others—a lot of R&B (especially Boyz II Men and Shai), but also old soul, like Stevie Wonder, the Temptations and Peabo Bryson. And then there's also the gospel of Take 6 and the Commissioned, which is really only one step away from R&B.

For a long, long time AJ's most precious possession was the blanket he'd been given when he was born. He carried it everywhere, not just when he was little, but even when he was older, even when he was a teenager, until he was fifteen, and on the road with the rest of the Boys in South Carolina. There, in a motel, the maid, thinking it was an old rag, took it from his room and put it in with the rest of the garbage. "I'm not over it," AJ admits. "I miss it like crazy, because it was my favorite blanket. Now it's gone for good."

But a lot happens to AJ when he's on tour. Some of it's good, but he always seems to attract some wildness to him. Once, in Europe, he had an earring literally ripped out of his ear. He was leaning over at the time to kiss a fan "and she put her finger through my hoop

and yanked it out.'' Not too surprisingly, for a while that
made him cautious about getting too close to fans, but
now he's happy to talk to them again, and sign autographs. In fact, of all the Boys, he's the one who's most
likely to just keep signing and signing, even after the
rest of the guys are ready to get going; he really appre-
ciates all that the fans have done for the band.
''. . . [W]hen we can, we like to give them some special
attention,'' he says. ''We're just trying to be nice and
give a little something back.''

He has had a few problems onstage, as he recalls: ''In
Germany someone threw a rock and it hit me in the face
during a performance. I thought it was a cuddly toy or
something. It caught me just above the eye. It was quite
a nasty cut. I had to carry on the show, though, as it was
part of a pop festival. If it had been our show, I would
have got security to find out who threw it!''

Then, in Montreal, when the Boys were appearing on
Musique Plus, the Quebecois version of Much Music,
Canada's MTV, he was caught in a crush as the band
was mobbed, ending up with a sprained ankle. Even with
that, he still performed, and later the soft cast (auto-
graphed by all the Boys) was auctioned off for charity
by a local radio station. No wonder that he's the guy
who admits he gets nervous before every song! With him
around, there's no telling what's going to happen next.

Give AJ a hotel room, and he can cause a little trouble,
even though he knows it'll all come back to him in the
long run. One time he broke a lamp, and he's thrown
fruit out of the windows at cars. Mostly, though, he's
''the king of hotels when it comes to not paying my bill.
I'll go through the mini bar, take all the Cokes and orange juices and tell them I've not had anything at all
when they ask the next morning. I do end up paying for
it in the long run. I got away with it for a while but then
they caught on.''

Their album goes platinum!

© Joe Major/London Features

© Pacha, Corbis

Kevin

© Marko Shark, Corbis

BRIAN

© Steve Granitz/Retna Ltd.

© Marko Shark, Corbis

Nick

© Pacha, Corbis

Howie

© Barbara Deliman/NGI

© Pacha, Corbis

© Pacha, Corbis

He's also the only one of the Boys who's expressed any interest in getting tattoos or piercings. He'd like to have his eyebrow pierced, and there are three tattoos he'd like, a big sun between his shoulderblades (now that would hurt!), his nickname, Bone, on his left arm, and the Japanese symbol for eternal life on his right arm. Will he have them done? This is AJ, after all . . . nothing's impossible. If he's in the right mood, he could come home sometime with all kinds of decoration on his body.

And that nickname of his, Bone. It came about when the guys were in Vienna, and AJ was shopping for jewelry. The stuff he really liked looked like bones and was meant to be Haitian voodoo symbols. His bodyguard began teasing AJ, telling him he was wearing bones, and combined with his skinny build, the name just stuck.

But his most recent acquisition is hardly bony, but a big one, in every way, a Rhodesian Ridgeback-boxer mix puppy, named Delilah.

"I was coming home from rehearsal one day," he explains, "and I should never have done it, but I stopped at the Humane Society for a look." Once he saw Delilah (her name came later, suggested by Brian), AJ was in love; he had to have her. And it seems as if Delilah is quite possessive of AJ, jealous of all the other girls interested in him. But, he says, "If it's any of my guy friends, she's all over them like a big flirt."

She might well have learned to flirt from her master, since AJ, by his own admission, is a master of it.

"If you want the biggest flirt, that's me," he admits. "I do flirt and I do like girls—I'm not going to say I don't." And he's also a real romantic. Because he was raised by his mom, AJ has definite respect for girls. "If I want to kiss [a girl], I'll say, 'Can I kiss you?' . . . I can't just move in, I have to ask, because if the girl's not comfortable, then I am not comfortable!"

He's the guy who'd be likely to take a date out to

McDonald's (which he jokingly refers to as Mack Daddy's) for dinner on a date. It's not because he's cheap, but because he wants to be able to show the real AJ, not to go all out to try and impress and be someone he's not (actually, since he's had some stomach problems, AJ is eating less greasy food these days, so Mickey D's might not end up on the menu).

And he doesn't want someone who's false, either. AJ's had enough heartbreak in his life. At the moment he doesn't have the time to settle into a real heavy-duty relationship, but he can see it in his future, although it would have to be someone "supportive of me and my career," and he would give her exactly the same respect in return. She'd have to be trustworthy, not another Melissa or Jennifer. And she'd need plenty going on in her own life, not be just sitting around always waiting for him, with goals and a career of her own. Most importantly, she would have to be "someone I can bring home to my mom."

What really attracts AJ, believe it or not, is eyes. He really doesn't care about physical type, but the eyes are important, "because if I could look deep past those eyes, it's like, 'Wow!'" and although he does find short hair attractive, like most of the Boys, he really prefers long hair on a girl. And a good, unpredictable sense of humor, to match his own, is important.

"I like funny girls who will pop in and say, 'Here I am!'" It doesn't matter what she looks like, though— honestly!"

The most fun he's had recording with BSB was at Fun Factory, when they were laying down "Get Down (You're The One For Me)," for their first album (it's also on their first American CD). Apart from being an excellent song, AJ feels it shows a whole other side of the band. "Toni [Cottura] the producer was really cool, a great writer," he says. "I think it shows we can rap a little bit, and it has more of that hip-hop sound."

But anything that showcases the Boys is all right with him. Even though touring can be grueling, he loves it, and feels there's nothing to compare with the rush of singing in front of their fans. It's the perfect job for him.

"I'm a big ham and I've got to be out there and doing stuff for no apparent reason, especially on stage," he says. But that's just the real AJ coming through.

He still lives at home with his mom, although he doesn't get to see her as much as he'd like to (she used to come on tour as a chaperone). They're very close, and he also keeps in frequent contact with his grandparents and his aunt and uncle. He's thought about getting an apartment, like Howie, Brian, and Kevin, but for the moment he just can't see the point. He's comfortable with his mom (who looks after Delilah while he's gone), and he really isn't home enough to make it worthwhile spending money on rent.

The big advantage of being gone so much (apart from seeing the fans) is that "my room at home is really tidy ... My keyboards are there, lots of Stephen King books, and my sound system."

BSB is the focus of his life; that's just the way it has to be for right now, and as far into the future as AJ can see, which is just fine with him. For all their success overseas, America is important to him; after all, it's where he's from. He's even learned to play the bass in order to improve the overall act, so he can join Kevin and Nick as instrumentalists onstage.

One place you wouldn't have found AJ until recently, however, is behind the wheel of a car. When he first took the test for his driver's license, he failed the written portion of the exam, and until the end the Boys were too busy for him to reschedule. When he finally did pass and get his license, the first thing he did was go out and treat himself to a car—in this case, a BMW 325i, with special wheels and low profile tires. That was cool for cruising around town, but for getting out into the country he needed something a little more rugged. Enter his new Tahoe truck, nicknamed the Silver Bullet because of its metallic silver color.

In his trademark sunglasses (and he really wouldn't object too much if a sunglasses company wanted to sponsor him, he jokes), AJ is as cool as they come. But don't be fooled. Underneath it all, he's just as much a regular guy as any of the others, with his hopes, dreams, and insecurities. He's had his share of bad luck, but now the Boys are huge everywhere, things are finally going his way. All his life he's been working toward something, just like Kevin, Howie, Brian, and Nick. He just didn't know that things could ever be this good. Becoming a star in America, on top of everywhere else, is the real cherry on the sundae. Before it all began to break here, AJ was the most nervous—but then again, he's notorious for worrying. "Even though this is home for us," he said at the time, "it's still a new territory and you don't know what the reaction will be."

He needn't have worried, although you couldn't tell him that. Once they got to know, America lapped up the Backstreet Boys the same as fans everywhere, and that deep bass voice of AJ's came booming out of radios and stereos everywhere. He's got the chance to be a ham for a whole new country of people, and it won't be long before the Boys are selling out arenas all over the U.S. And they'll be doing it for a long time to come yet. As long as AJ doesn't have any more accidents, that is!

♪ NICK ♪

If any one of the Backstreet Boys seemed destined from birth for a career in show business, it was Nicholas Gene Carter. When you're born in the same hospital as comedienne Lucille Ball (*I Love Lucy*), it's almost inevitable. So it's no surprise that's what happened with Nick.

Robert and Jane Carter owned a restaurant and lounge in Westfield, New York, just outside Jamestown. Called the Yankee Rebel, it was a lot of hard work for them, from early morning to late at night, but business was good, especially after they installed a video arcade room to the side of the restaurant. Since they lived upstairs, they were at least close to the place.

Their first child, Nicholas Gene Carter, was born on January 28, 1980, and it was as if the spirit of Lucille Ball was in him. As soon as he could crawl, he was an entertainer, charming the customers in the restaurant. When he was two, and walking, he managed to vanish downstairs by himself. When Jane, who was cleaning the family's apartment, began looking for him, he was nowhere to be found! Frantic, she went downstairs to get her husband searching. And there was Nick, in the arcade, playing video games while a couple of women fed him quarters to keep him going! They were amused by what he was doing, so Nick was happy. And once she'd found him, Jane was, too.

Nick was a cute kid, but a little funny-looking, too (although he obviously grew out of that!).

"My family used to call me Charlie Brown," he admits, " 'cause I had a big round head and no hair. There's still baby pictures of me on display at home, which is a bit embarrassing. My mom's even got the family album out when a girl's been round and gone, 'Here's a picture of Nick as a baby without any clothes on!' "

He didn't stay an only child for long. When he was two, Nick was joined by a sister, Bobbie Jean, whom everyone in the family immediately began calling BJ. A year after that came Lesley, and then the twins, Aaron and Angel, to round things out at five kids.

But by the time the twins arrived, everything had changed in the Carter family. Jamestown had its attractions, but weather wasn't one of them. Bitterly cold in the winter, then steaming with humidity in the summer, it wasn't the best place in the world to live. On vacations, Robert and Jane had taken their family to Florida. They liked the life down there, the way it seemed a little slower, the idea of living by the water, and most of all the fact that they wouldn't have to spend the winters digging out from several feet of snow!

The idea of moving to Florida slowly became more and more attractive. Selling the Yankee Rebel would give them a good stake to start over, enough to get a nice house—someplace bigger than an apartment over a business, which was starting to get cramped as the family grew—a place where the kids could really play, and enjoy a better life than their parents.

Finally it was decided, and the restaurant and lounge went up for sale. Once a deal was done, the Carters packed up the car and headed south, to Ruskin, Florida, just outside Tampa Bay.

Robert and Jane already had a place picked out, a house close to the water, with a pool in the backyard.

To them this was their American dream, living where they wanted, in a place that seemed perfect.

Nick, who was four, immediately took to Ruskin. The sunshine and the warmth year-round felt great to him. He'd been outgoing when he lived up North, but now it was as if the sun really made him blossom.

Still energetic, and a bit of a prankster (a trait he'd really develop in BSB), he seemed to love to perform. Singing, dancing, acting parts from the movies his parents took him to see, if it involved doing something in front of other people, Nick was interested.

Jane, however, thought it was just a childhood phase, that he'd grow out of it and become a "regular" kid. At least, she thought that until he was nine years old. Nick was still the ham, ready to entertain any audience; it didn't even have to be people.

"I used to stand on a tree stump in our back garden and sing, pretending the flowers were my audience," he recalls. "One day my mom caught me and enrolled me in singing lessons straight away."

At that point, Jane Carter could deny it no longer— Nick had been born to do this!

Singing lessons were just the start. Soon Nick was ready to perform in public, and he made his debut in a local production of "The Phantom of the Opera." For his age he had a remarkable voice, very mature and strong, but capable of putting a lot of emotion across. As soon as "Phantom" closed, he was ready for more— now he'd had a taste of the stage, he was hungry for it all.

So Jane took her ten-year-old son down to an audition, to sing during the Tampa Bay Buccaneers' halftime show. To her surprise, Nick got the job, and for the next two seasons, he was there every other Sunday, out on the football field, singing to thousands and thousands of people.

Even that didn't seem to satisfy him. It was great

when he was rehearsing or out in front of the crowds, but that wasn't all the time. And so Jane began taking him to auditions for other jobs, to talent shows, anywhere Nick could get up and sing. At twelve, he entered and won the Universal New Original Amateur Hour, another feather in his cap.

By then, however, he'd started working with Nickelodeon and the Disney Channel. Nick had the kind of talent and enthusiasm they liked, even if he did have the audacity to turn down a Disney role, because he felt it just wasn't right for him. He'd taken part in a couple of commercials and there was talk of casting him in a series—in fact, it was at an audition that he met AJ, then Howie, and soon the three of them were singing, just to pass the time as they waited, and it didn't take long before they realized they sounded pretty good together.

If there was one worry about Nick's involvement with BSB, it wasn't his talent—that was obvious!—but his age. When the Boys began, he was still only thirteen, and Robert and Jane were very worried about his education. But once the tutors had been arranged, and his parents realized that Nick could possibly end up with a better education than he'd get in school, everything was settled. At first, Robert Carter went on the road with the Boys, to look after his son, and make sure he was being treated well. But once he saw everything was in order, he was happy to let the managers take control of everything. And that's the way it's been ever since. Now Nick is eighteen, and just finishing his high school courses, a good student who hasn't been allowed to slack off, even when the Boys have been touring all over the world. It's a demanding schedule, but it's paid off in every way. The biggest thrill he's had in the band, and there have been many, has been "to actually walk into a store and see your single sitting on a shelf. You can't believe it's you sitting next to all these other famous artists."

As everyone knows, Nick is the youngest of the Boys,

two years younger than AJ, and almost eight years younger than Kevin, the eldest. But, at five feet eleven inches ("and still growing") he's definitely not the smallest. The fans have seen him grow up right before their eyes. He started out cute and cuddly, but he's gone on to develop into a real hunk, just like the other guys.

Although he looks all grown up on the outside, the real Nick still has a lot of the kid in him. When the boys are home, the first thing he does, he admits, is go to his little brother's room, "to play with all his toys. I start off with his Sega then move right on down, finishing with my favorite toys of the lot—his Ninja Turtle models! I spend hours re-enacting key scenes and I get soooo upset when anyone interferes."

Well, why not? The other thing Nick really loves to do in his very precious free time is to be in the water. Every morning he'll do his laps in the pool behind the family's home. But that's not the extent of his swimming. Nick's real hobby is scuba diving.

"My parents taught me to dive," he explains. "They started to explore the sea as a hobby several years ago." For Nick, the fascination began with the dolphins who'd swim in the channel behind their property that led up from the Gulf of Mexico.

". . . [T]hey swam past our house and they were totally tame," he says. "They even let you touch them. Eventually, I wanted to swim along with them."

At that point he knew he wanted to learn how to scuba, although he had no idea how difficult it would be to become certified, which would allow him to go down in open water. First he had to learn the theory, hours of it, with plenty of homework. After that, the new divers began in a swimming pool, getting familiar with all the equipment, and comfortable using it in all kinds of situations.

But Nick persisted, and eventually passed his certificate, and he thinks it was worth all the time and effort.

"When you find out how to move yourself along, it's just like floating," he says with awe. And it's freedom, the chance to explore a whole new world. Even now, though, Nick doesn't go too deep, usually only about ten meters, where there's plenty of wild life to see, and the deepest he's gone is only forty meters. But it is, he says, the coolest thing.

And even when he's not in a mood for going under it, the waters of the Gulf of Mexico still attract him, and he might well get in the Carter family speedboat and take off for a few hours. Even his favorite place in the world—the Florida Keys—is surrounded by water.

Among the Boys, it's Nick who's acquired the reputation as the band's jokester. And it's really deserved, since, he admits, "I like to do anything I can think of to these guys."

According to Howie, Nick's that way because of his age.

"He's full of energy when he wants to be, but he doesn't always know how to focus this energy. . . ."

There was the time he snuck all AJ's clothes from his hotel room while AJ was sleeping. Or the cake fight he started at a party. And it hasn't just been the guys, either. Nick was the one who slipped manager Donna Wright a piece of very strange chewing gum that he'd come across, not bothering it to tell her that it tasted of fish!

Of course, everything comes around, and the Boys have had their revenge on Nick for all his pranks.

"Once, we threw him out of the dressing room in his underwear in front of a whole bunch of girls," recalls a laughing Brian. "He got real mad but it was really funny!"

Brian, of course, is Nick's closest bud in the band, Frick to Nick's Frack. They often room together on the road, and there's a strong bond between them. As Brian says, "I don't expect him to give me respect just because

I'm older—I don't have those sort of power trips! It's a totally equal thing.''

Even when they argue, as they sometimes do over their ongoing Mario Kart competition, it never lasts long, according to Brian. They might get mad at each other, ''Then a couple of minutes later, it's like, 'Hey, Frick,' then, 'Wassup, Frack?' and it's cool.''

But it's not just with Brian that Nick's an equal. That applies throughout the band.

''I've got just as equal a part in the band as the other four. That's what this group's all about—we decide on everything we do, from which record we're going to release, to what direction we're going in. We're all shareholders in our company, so everything is up to us.''

But the rest of the guys do take care of him.

''[W]e all look out for each other. They're always there to give me advice. They've already been through most of the things I'm going through, so they can help me like that and, hey, they're always there to talk to— they're my brothers!''

Like all the others, Nick has a passion for basketball. But there's something else he does, which is spend a lot of time drawing. You're likely to find him backstage while the Boys wait around with a pen and some paper, doing cartoons of everyone. He's even come up with the idea of a Backstreet Boys comic book, which he's now finished! ''I'm looking for someone to put my ideas down on paper,'' he says, ''as I just don't get enough time to do all the illustrations myself.''

He loves art, and if he were ever to go to college, that would be his major, although he does admit that ''I'd mainly like to play basketball.''

It might be hard to believe, but the cute one was never popular when he was in school.

''I was very different from the others, and I was away from class a lot . . . so the guys never liked me. I never got any of the beautiful girls, either! I guess the girl-friends I had were nice, but they weren't amazingly gorgeous. They weren't the cheerleader types." Those types, he remembers, "weren't interested in me. They were only interested in dating the cool Italian or Spanish dudes, and I was like, 'Hey, give me a try,' but they never did."

And now they're probably really regretting being so stuck-up.

In fact, Nick has a very mature, down-to-earth view of himself. A lot of girls might think he's perfect, but he knows full well that he's not. "I'm a normal human being, and so are the other guys, and I make mistakes and they make mistakes and I just try to live my life to the fullest. I try to have fun, and that is all I'm doing right now."

Away from the Boys, the biggest thing in his life, by far, is his family. They're all very close, and as the eldest he feels a strong responsibility toward his brothers and sisters. At eighteen, he definitely doesn't feel ready to leave home yet (although these days he doesn't see too much of Ruskin any more). Besides, if he did, he said, he'd have to take care of the cooking, cleaning, and laundry, and he doesn't want to deal with that.

Of all the guys, Nick probably has the widest musical tastes. Not only does he love R&B, but all kinds of sounds, from the alternative guitars of Nirvana to the Eighties stadium rock of Journey—believe it or not—mostly because he loves vocalist Steve Perry's voice.

And, unlike the others, Nick has never had a really serious relationship. He's had his share of girlfriends, but the emphasis has always been much more on *friends*.

"To be honest," he admits, "I've never really fallen in love. I've never felt this strong sensation." Of course, there are plenty of girls in love with him—of all the Boys, he's the one who gets mobbed the most—but right now he doesn't have the time for romance in his life.

The Backstreet Boys are just too busy, and it wouldn't be right to start something and then have to leave to go on tour. Even when he dated a girl for a long time, nearly a year, it wasn't a full-on romance, although it seemed like it at the time.

Her name was Bryn, and Nick met her when they were both taking part in a production of "Annie Get Your Gun."

"Me and this other guy both liked her, so she had to choose," he recalls. "One night I waited backstage, and when she came back I kissed her. So I won the girl and we went out for a year."

Nor is he in any hurry to fall in love. As he rightly points out, "I've got my whole life ahead of me to worry about that."

Still, none of that stops him thinking about his ideal girl. She'd need to be quite tall, just a little shorter than him, and preferably with long dark hair—exactly the opposite of Nick's blondness (his favorite movie star is Christina Ricci, if that gives you any clues). And above all, she'd have to love him for who he is, not for the fact that he's a Backstreet Boy. Obviously, she'd also need a really good sense of humor, as Nick doesn't seem likely to stop playing his practical jokes anytime soon. Also, since he's a guy who likes a challenge, always agreeing to do what he wants to do isn't a good idea. She'd need to be quite determined. And faithful, since he could never date someone who was seeing another guy. But in return, you'd know he was going to be true, since he "could never see any other girls besides my girlfriend."

But he is one of the Boys who admits that he would date a fan, even if he thinks it probably won't go any further than dating (but you never know, do you?).

Nor would Nick mind if a girl asked him out; in fact, he'd like it. "I like girls asking you out, 'cause it takes the pressure out of you having to do it!"

Above everything else, though, she had to enjoy hugs. "I need a hug every day," Nick says. "I get lots of hugs from the fans and the guys, but I don't get a proper hug—I wish I did!"

His perfect romantic evening with a girl would in the place he calls "paradise," the Florida Keys, the two of them picnicking on a beach as the sun set and the stars came out, then maybe going for a ride in a boat, which all sounds pretty good.

Onstage you're going to see Nick behind the drums a little bit—and maybe more to come. When he was eleven, he began taking lessons on the instrument, as if he didn't already have enough to do with his time, and he's kept at it, until he's now good enough to play along with Kevin (and now AJ) in concert. In the future, he can see himself doing more drumming, too, and maybe even playing some rock.

He loves the life he has (and who wouldn't?), and he's really committed to the Backstreet Boys. It's his dream. "We wanted to make it happen and that is what we did," he says seriously. "And we enjoy every minute of it and we take every day like it's our last."

There are two Nicks, really. Around the Boys and the fans, he likes to cute it up a little bit, but around adults, his maturity really shines through. He's already paid off his parents' house with the money he's made; he can be very responsible, not the type to be wild and get into trouble.

"I've never been drunk," he says. "I'm under age, so I'd get myself in trouble if I drank. It's never interested me. I've heard from some people that drinking isn't bad for your health if you keep it in moderation, but personally I don't like it."

But apart from being a good role model, he's happiest if he can spend a lot of his time just playing Nintendo games (his *favorite* pastime on the road), or being at home around his family, and playing with the Carters' golden retriever, Simba, named for the character in Disney's *The Lion King*. If he wants solitude, he'll just slip on his scuba gear and vanish into the water for a while.

It's a little bit unfortunate, given the amount of traveling the Boys do between continents, but Nick really hates to fly. And if that has to happen in the morning, then things couldn't be worse, because Nick *really* isn't a morning person. Catch him before lunch and you won't be seeing cute Nick, but some grumpy imitator.

Everything has happened very quickly for Nick, and while he's still very young. A lot of people would have let the fame go to their heads, but everyone else has helped keep his feet on the ground.

"I'm proud of the way he handles everything that comes along and how he's matured," says Brian. "Nick's always real straight-faced and gets the job done the best he can."

And Nick himself agrees that the experience of being in the band has helped him grow up well.

"I mean, I am three years older than when we started," he says, "so there are certainly going to be changes in my personality . . . But you know, I still feel like a kid in a lot of ways."

He got the chance to indulge the kid when all the boys went out car shopping, buying himself a bright green pickup truck equipped with *everything*—huge stereo, oversize tires, and sport wheels. That wasn't the end of it, though. A truck wasn't enough for Nick. While he was out, he also picked up a brand new Corvette! Way to go!

Of course, international stardom has meant a loss of privacy, not only for Nick himself, but also for his family. At Christmas 1996, fans showed up at his door right as the family was sitting down to eat Christmas dinner. He ended up standing outside signing autographs (the fans came back the next day to apologize for disturbing the Carters on a holiday, then wrote Nick to say meeting him had been their Christmas present). Someone in Tampa even decided to make a quick buck giving guided tours to Nick's home, filling chartered buses and driving to the place, where the visitors could get out and take photographs. His Dad finally had to put a fence around the property because girls were digging up flowers and pieces of the lawn to take home as souvenirs. And one time, at a concert, a girl held up a poster, a picture of Nick's house, and she'd written on it, "I was there." He looked down and said, "My house is in the audience!"

When he's at home (and not beseiged by fans), Robert and Jane treat Nick like any of their other kids. "I have to do a lot of baby-sitting and I have chores," Nick explains. "You know, the usual things, washing dishes and taking out the garbage, that kind of stuff." But he really doesn't mind; he's back home with his family, the place he loves best in all the world.

♪ PART TWO ♪

THE BAND

It's no secret that the Backstreet Boys are the most happening band in America right now. But it took us more than two years to catch up on what the rest of the world had already figured out—that these five guys singing harmony could be not only gorgeous to look at, but sing like angels.

Of course, that means we've got a lot of catching up to do. Backstreet is definitely back in the U.S. now. They've toured, just astounding fans all over with their show, and their album and the "Quit Playing Games (With My Heart)" single have both gone platinum, a pretty good indication that this country is finally ready for them.

But it wasn't always that way. When the guys first put it all together, America really wasn't interested in them (foolish us). That was in 1993. Back then, it was alternative that was huge. Sure, Boyz II Men could score hits, but New Edition, New Kids on the Block, and Color Me Badd, who all used harmonies, had folded. The closest anyone came to what the Boys were doing was in R&B, which was very separate from the pop field.

What mainstream radio wanted at the time was alternative. It had broken through in 1991 with Nirvana and Pearl Jam, and it was still going strong. Hip-hop was coming on strong, and, of course, Michael Jackson could do no wrong in terms of sales. Which isn't to say pop music wasn't around; it was, and always will be. But there was no big, big band that teenagers could identify with. Pop music wasn't getting respect, and it wouldn't until the Spice Girls came over to America and gave the country a kick and Girl Power.

It was an idea whose time had come again. After years of angst and gangsta rap, America was ready for pop music again. There was Hanson, and now, even better, there are the Backstreet Boys.

In the rest of the world, though, pop music had never gone away. Alternative had come and gone, and made its mark, as had hip-hop, and dance music. But they shared the charts with pop. Maybe it's the difference in attitude, but most places didn't have the same stuck-up attitude toward pop. As long as it was good—like Backstreet—people wanted to listen to it. And that's the way it should be. Quite a few years ago, George Michael had released an album called *Listen Without Prejudice,* which was some very sound advice, and that was what America needed to do, to copy its cousins around the globe.

Once that finally started to happen, mostly because people realized that teenagers wanted to hear music, too, the success of the Backstreet Boys was inevitable. They weren't rock stars in leather, doing drugs, or rappers killing each other. They were genuine, nice guys, the kind your mom would be glad if you brought home. They dressed like regular guys, and looked like them—no weirdness. And that, ironically, made them stand out.

It's taken a long time, and a lot of work, but America understands the Backstreet magic now. But let's see how the whole story unfolded. . . .

♪ *1993-1995* ♪

Really, we have Nickelodeon to thank for the Backstreet Boys. If the television network for kids hadn't started, and located its studios in Orlando, they might never have got together, and the world would be a much poorer place today.

"We were always auditioning for Nickelodeon shows," Howie says of himself and AJ. Having been introduced by a vocal coach at a talent competition (the coach AJ used, who'd previously been Howie's coach), once they began seeing each other at auditions, it was only natural that they'd begin singing together, a capella, to pass the time they had to wait.

Nick Carter was also going to the auditions, and one day he began singing with Howie and AJ. At first it was for fun, more a laugh than anything else. Soon, though, the trio began to realize that they sounded pretty good together on the Boyz II Men, Color Me Badd songs, and old R&B hits they were covering. Maybe it was possible to make something of this. The only way was to find out.

None of the boys were strangers to show business, and they weren't shy about performing in public. Three guys together, singing, though, didn't mean much. What they needed was a record.

And that was why they took their vocalizing to all the record labels in Orlando.

"We'd go to local labels and sing a capella in their foyers," Howie recalls. "We'd sing anywhere, for anybody."

At first, it didn't seem to do any good. No one was interested. Besides Boyz II Men, no one was interested in harmony groups any more, particularly if they were made up of teenagers. It would have been easy to have become discouraged, and for Howie, AJ, and Nick to have given up. But they were absolutely certain they had something special, and they knew that if they connected with the right person, things would begin to happen.

So when they heard of a new record label starting up, they made an appointment, and went down. The label was Transcontinental Records, and it was owned by Louis J. Pearlman, known to everybody as Lou, the man the guys would come to call "Big Poppa."

"He was looking for talent so we went in and auditioned for him," says Howie.

He heard them, and he didn't say that he wasn't interested. He liked the harmonies, and he saw the potential—enough to have them record a demo tape. That was hardly a record deal, or even a guarantee of one. But it was a beginning, and one step further than they'd been before.

Still, Lou realized something was missing in the sound. These guys could definitely sing, but it needed to be fuller, to cover more range. What they really needed was two more voices; that would fill it out perfectly.

There were plenty of teenagers who were auditioning for shows in Orlando, and by now Howie, AJ, and Nick knew a lot of them. Some had great voices, so after talking it through, two of the guys were approached about joining the band.

As a five-piece, the difference in their sound was tremendous. Fuller, richer, everything Lou had hoped. He signed them to Transcontinental, and suggested they get themselves a manager.

They were ready to take that next step, and do just that, when the group fell apart. The two new guys weren't happy with the situation; they didn't like the type of R&B material the guys were singing, and quit.

That seemed to take everything back to square one—but only for a few days. Lou was discussing the new situation with a friend of his, who just happened to know someone—a very good singer—who was currently working at Disneyworld. He'd give him a call and have him come down and try out for the band. The singer's name was Kevin Richardson. He appeared for the audition, sang with the others—who were becoming very professional together—and fit like a glove.

"There were two other members who didn't work out and I replaced them," Kev says. They briefly thought about working as a quartet, but that fifth voice would make all the difference. "Then we needed another member," Kevin continues. "Brian's my cousin ... and I called him up and he came down to Florida ... and he auditioned."

The five couldn't have sounded more perfect together if they'd been rehearsing for a year. *This* was a band. Like any band, they needed a name, and finally settled on Backstreet Boys, naming themselves after Orlando's Backstreet Market, a famous place locally, where tourists, teens, everybody used to hang out.

"It was a flea market," Kevin explains, "but when there was no flea market, there was a big parking lot. That was where the kids would drive their cars, hang out with their convertibles, and listen to music. That's how we got Backstreet. We put Boys on it, because no matter how old we get we'll always be boys."

So now they had all their members, a name, and a recording contract. The next thing they needed was a manager, who'd be able to get them singing in front of people.

By 1993, with Disney, MGM, Universal, and Nickelodeon, Orlando had become quite a center of the entertainment industry. So it was no big surprise that some powerful managers had relocated down there into the sunshine to do business. One company that had made the move was the Wright Stuff, owned by Donna Wright and her husband Johnny. In the late Eighties and early Nineties they'd been one of the top managers in music, having guided the careers of both New Edition and then New Kids on the Block, the two biggest singing groups in recent memory. What they didn't know about handling groups like that wasn't worth knowing. Guys who could sing and dance, and who were also decidedly cute, were their specialty. If anyone could help the Backstreet Boys become big, and fulfill their potential, it was the Wrights.

Lou Pearlman knew that, and he knew Johnny and Donna. He called them, and suggested they come and listen to his new signings. It only took a few songs before they were convinced that the guys were going to be massive.

"My whole career, I've always gone on instinct," Donna Wright explains. "When I first heard the Backstreet Boys, I got the chills so strong that the hairs just stood up straight on the back of my neck. I could just tell there was something there."

The Wrights could see the potential in BSB, but they knew the business well enough to understand that releasing a record straight off wasn't the right strategy. In 1993, the market in America wasn't ready for the Backstreet Boys. And, good as they were, the Boys weren't ready to go for the big time yet. They needed songs, and they needed moves.

AJ, in particular, was able to help with working out the choreography, the stage dances for the Boys. And for songs, they already had the covers of Shai, Jodeci, Boyz II Men, and Color Me Badd that they'd worked up. It was a case of putting it all together.

They did that over the course of several months' intensive rehearsal in Florida. The Boys, Lou, the Wrights—none of them were looking at this in the short-term. They could be huge, but it would take time, and a lot of work.

Backstreet were also going to need performing experience. So far they'd sung together, they could all dance together, but apart from when they were auditioning to try and get a record deal, they'd never really played in front of an audience.

The best way to do that, and build a fan base at the same time, was the tried-and-trusted grass roots circuit. That entailed going to every high school and mall that would have them, and putting on a show. For music they used backing tapes. It was just the boys onstage, doing what they did best—entertaining. To help recoup some of the costs, they recorded a single with Lou for Transcontinental, "Tell Me That I'm Dreaming," which they sold at shows.

And, to their amazement, a talent scout from Mercury Records caught one of their shows, and signed the Boys, via Transcontinental, to a deal with the label. This was great, exactly what they'd hoped!

"With a band like this, it's all about marketing," Johnny Wright said in 1997. "That's why we went to all those schools, performed at school assemblies, and signed autographs for sixteen- and seventeen-year-old girls. We wanted the Boys to be accessible to their fans, to meet them one on one."

As a strategy, it worked. It was a case of winning over fans, one by one. It wasn't easy, and the daily grind of traveling and performing (and for Brian, AJ, and Nick, of also having to study while they were on the road) was exhausting. But it was worth every minute. They were making new friends and fans all over the South, in every place they performed.

And the word was spreading about them, too. A girl

who'd seen them and loved what they did would tell a friend who went to another school, and soon a lot of people who'd never actually heard them would know who they were. So when the Boys came back through the area, there'd be more schools to play, which would lead to more fans.

Initially they were playing in the South, but as their reputation grew, the net widened. Within a matter of months, as 1993 turned in 1994, they had real hardcore fans, and were performing all over the eastern half of the country. The people who saw them weren't just being polite, either, and clapping when a song was finished. By now the Boys were polished and confident in their singing and dancing, and they got their fans screaming for them.

What they needed, and soon, was a record, but Mercury was showing no signs of putting them in the studio. In fact, they let the option expire without ever recording them. Everything was back to square one. BSB were still signed to Lou's Transcontinental label, but he knew Transcontinental couldn't do what was needed to make them stars all across America; his label just didn't have the distribution, or the money to spend on advertising. So the plan he devised with the Wrights and the Boys was for another label to release their records, which would still be under the auspices of Transcontinental, with Lou as exective director of the projects.

The only immediate problem was that no label seemed to be interested. What the Boys were doing wasn't happening in the charts, and no major record executive believed things were likely to change anytime soon. Certainly, there wasn't enough faith for anyone to take a gamble on signing them, and maybe lose a whole bunch of money.

About the only label that had shown real curiosity was Jive, based in Florida, and that was largely because David McPherson, the man who'd signed them to Mercury, was now vice president of artists and repertoire at the label. Jive had enjoyed big success from unlikely things in the past, most notably DJ Jazzy Jeff and the Fresh Prince, back in the 1980s, the kind of hip-hop duo no one had thought would sell in mass quantities. But they had, with hit singles, multiplatinum albums, and the start of a career as a megastar for the Fresh Prince, better known to everyone now by his real name, Will Smith.

But even Jive wasn't convinced enough to offer the Backstreet Boys a record contract. They needed real proof of the Boys' popularity first.

That was where Ohio entered the picture. By now the Boys had fans—major fans—that far North. They'd been through the area several times, and each visit drew bigger and louder crowds. Now they were back in Columbus, and the reaction was just going way over the top. Girls were yelling for them, loud enough to drown out any of the singing, and Donna Wright had an inspiration. She took out her cell phone, and called the executive at Jive who was still considering signing the Boys to the label. After they'd talked for a minute, according to AJ, she "basically held the phone up to [capture] the reaction of the crowd of kids, who were screaming and going crazy and everything. . . ."

That was basically all Jive needed to know. Any band who could get fans going like that, without even having a real record out, had to be something special. As soon as the band returned to Florida, Jive brought them in to audition, and to hear them sing a capella, to make sure they really could do it.

Of course, there was no problem with that. The Boys had been singing that way for over a year now, and they passed the test with flying colors. Within a month of Donna's concert call to the label, the Backstreet Boys signed a record contract with Jive.

*   *   *

Things were definitely moving along. The Boys had a fan base, and now they had a record deal. All they had to do was to connect the two. What they needed, though, was the right song. In concert they'd been covering the hits of other groups, which just wouldn't cut it for a record of their own. Kevin had written songs, as had Brian, and Howie, but nothing that was really suitable for BSB, and certainly not for the first "real" BSB single. That needed to be something so catchy, so addictive, that everyone would sit up and take notice.

Jive and the Wrights contacted writers they knew, and songs began to appear. However, good as they were, there was nothing that quite caught anyone's ear as that magical first single.

Then they started looking further afield. One of the biggest, and most irresistible, singles of early 1994 was "The Sign" by Ace of Base, a Swedish group. They'd already had one big U.S. single, "All That She Wants." Their producer, Denniz PoP, was contacted. He hadn't written the hit, but with his writing partners, Max Martin and Herbert Crichlow, he did have some songs up his sleeve. With a few alterations to the lyrics, one of them, called "We've Got It Goin' On" would be perfect for the Boys. It would give them a chance to showcase their harmonies, it had a great dance beat, a rap, and a chorus that stuck in the mind like Velcro. If anything was going to establish the Backstreet Boys, this was the song. It put all the best things about BSB into one small package.

And the person to record it was Denniz PoP. He was still hot from Ace of Base, who'd follow up their American Number One with a third hit, "Don't Turn Around." Arrangements were made to fly the Boys over to Stockholm, Sweden, where PoP had his Cheiron Studios.

Even though Kevin, Howie, Brian, AJ, and Nick hadn't made a record yet, this was like a dream come true. Not only *was* there going to be a record, they got to travel to Europe to make it. For five guys who'd never set foot outside America, this was truly exciting.

1994 was becoming 1995 as they settled in Stockholm. The city was covered in snow, looking like a picture postcard. But there wasn't much chance for the Boys to play tourist in Sweden. They were there to work. PoP, Martin, and Crichlow had been busy. Backstreet wouldn't just be recording "We've Got It Goin' On" but three songs. PoP and Martin had written "I Wanna Be With You," while Martin and Crichlow had put their pens together to come up with "Quit Playing Games (With My Heart)." The Boys, who had an equal say with Lou and the Wrights on what material they recorded, were blown away by all three songs, and it was decided to extend the sessions in Stockholm to get all three of them on tape.

Considering this was their first time in a real studio, the sessions went incredibly smoothly. But why wouldn't they? The Boys were all professionals, and very seasoned professionals by now, having spent a full year on the high school circuit. They were used to each other's voices, and how they worked best together. And they were also fully used to being away from home together.

"At first you had to learn what would set everybody off," Kevin says. "But now it's like family. I never had a little brother, but now I've got four. We don't get along perfectly. We have our arguments, but they get worked out."

Still, it took a little time to get everything just right. Perfection was what everyone was aiming for, on the harmonies, on the raps. But when the guys settled in the control room to hear the final mixes blasting through the speakers, they knew it was worth all the time, and the weariness of singing take after take after take. They all believed that each of the songs had hit written all over it.

Being away from home over Christmas had been difficult, particularly for Nick, the youngest of the group, but the end result more than made up for the separation from their families. Backstreet was definitely going to be happening.

Back home in America, it was time for a little vacation. The Boys had been working solidly for over a year and a half without a break, every day intense, whether it was rehearsing, performing, traveling, or recording. They'd come a long, long way, and the journey was only just beginning. For now they needed a little time to themselves, to recharge their batteries, and get ready for the big push toward chart success.

For Kev and Brian, that meant flying to Lexington, to relax with their families, and tell them everything that had happened to them. Howie stayed in Orlando. AJ didn't have too much to tell his mom, since she'd spent a lot of the time on the road with them. With no other children, she was free to travel with the band and act as an overall surrogate parent and chaperone, making sure they—and AJ, in particular—didn't get into *too* much trouble. Nick went home to Ruskin, to spend time with his younger brothers and sisters, do some scuba diving (there hadn't exactly been too much chance for that in the freezing waters of Stockholm in winter!), and take the boat out in the Bay.

Until they finally disembarked from the plane in sunny Florida, none of the guys had realized how tired they were. The last two years, from getting together to making a record, had gone by in one tremendous rush, a blur of cities and faces.

Of course it had all been a buzz. But it had only been the prelude. Bigger and better was just around the corner.

The Boys, as well as the Wrights and Lou Pearlman, had their sights very firmly set on America. Conquering the country wouldn't be easy, but with patience and a lot of effort, they could manage it. All the touring in high schools, malls, all those small places they'd played and won fans, would pay off when their record appeared. They were offering America sweet pop music, with more than a hint of R&B, and the kind of tempo they could dance to. Maybe harmony groups weren't the most popular commodity in the U.S. at the moment, but there was nothing to say they couldn't change that. They'd worked long and hard enough; everyone involved was totally committed to the band, and making it into a success story. The chemistry between Howie, AJ, Nick, Kev, and Brian was incredible, and they'd got enough live experience now to be charismatic on stage and really communicate with an audience. With a look, one of them could single out a girl in the crowd and sing directly to her. They had that elusive commodity known as star quality, and once "We've Got It Goin' On" hit the stores, everyone else would be forced to realize it, too.

For now, though, they could catch their breath, take a few weeks to calm down and become themselves again, before it all began in even more frenzied fashion. Kevin came back to Florida, to Orlando, and spent some time in the apartment with Howie, before Brian returned to join them.

The warm weather felt good, relaxing. They could drive to the coast and hang by the beach, or just sit by the pool in their apartment complex. They were going to be stars, but no one else knew that yet, so they were undisturbed by fans seeking them out. It would be the last time they'd have such peace at home.

Finally it was time to get together again. It was time for the Boys to do some more recording. By now they had acquired a number of new songs, mostly from those solicited for that first single. The guys had already spent time rehearsing the material, and they used two studios in Orlando, Parc and Platinum Post, to lay a lot of their vocals lines on top of the instrumentation. "Get Down

(You're The One For Me)," "I'll Never Break Your Heart," "Boys Will Be Boys," "Just To Be Close To You," "Every Time I Close My Eyes," "Darlin'," and "Roll with It" were all done there, with some additional tracking and mixing done at Battery and Wolfshead Studios up in Chicago.

All the Boys had been writing, but none of their songs were recorded; they weren't ready yet. Instead the material came from a variety of writers to complement the sides recorded in Sweden, a mix of ballads and uptempo pieces, all geared to suit the harmonies, and give each of the guys a chance to shine on lead vocals.

By summer it was time. "We've Got It Goin' On," the Backstreet Boys' first single, appeared on Jive Records.

There was a lot riding on one release for BSB. Jive and the Wrights had invested a lot of money in them, money that could only be repaid by a hit. Which meant this single had to do well. First it would be released in the U.S., where everyone believed the Boys had a chance of becoming big, and then in Europe.

When "We've Got It Goin' On" entered the *Billboard* Hot 100, it was as if everything was going to plan, and that dreams really were coming true in September 1996. It climbed slowly, but it *was* climbing.

Backstreet were doing all they could to support the record and make it into a success. They were touring, playing clubs and theaters this time, small venues, but in the areas they'd played before, where they had fans.

Of course, there was also a video. Putting a record out without one was pretty much like commercial suicide. This, as it should have been, was totally Backstreet, and filmed in Florida. It showed them performing in a club, on a small stage before an adoring audience, highlighting the dance moves they'd worked out for the song. There were snippets of them in the studio, singing around a microphone.

Then there was the guys outside, dressed—a little surprisingly, maybe—in black leather and denim, singing the song, with Brian's lead standing out, and AJ showing he was really down with the rap.

But the best part was the black and white "home movie" footage of Brian and Nick. They were washing Brian's Jeep (with its famous B-Rok license plate), helped by a friendly girl, then snuck off to join in a pickup game of b-ball on the court next door.

Of course, the two of them—Brian naturally wearing his Kentucky Wildcats shirt—beat all the rest of the guys, before trying to sneak back to work, as if they'd never been away, with Brian getting a face full of water from the hose for shirking.

It gave a good, rounded picture of the guys, showing they could sing, dance, that they looked great, and that they were real people too—in other words, everything that was intended.

And still the record climbed slowly, a month after its release.

Now it was time for "We've Got It Goin' On" to come out in Europe. The label believed that it could do really well in Britain, with its history of supporting boy bands. Take That was still the biggest thing there since sliced bread, East 17 was going strong—there was room for some American competition.

The European launch party for "We've Got It Goin' On" took place at Planet Hollywood in London. The Boys sang a capella for the assembled journalists, photographers, and public relations people. They loved to sing every opportunity they got, and since they'd started out singing a capella, it was second nature to them—and a part of their stage show. Above all, it proved they were real, that they really *could* sing and deliver the goods, that they weren't just another manufactured group. They followed it up with their first televised appearance a week later, on a variety show, followed by their first-ever press, in the magazine *Live and Kicking*, as the guys set off on their first British tour, with PJ and Duncan. It looked as if the Boys were going to do well in Britain.

These days, it's a song that holds a lot of very fond memories for them, although, Nick says, "Back then we had no idea it would be a hit. It seems so long ago."

In America, the single reached #69 and seemed to stall. The next week it didn't go up, and the week after that it began to fall. Things weren't looking good at home.

Europe, though, was a different story altogether. From the day it hit the stores, the record was popular. In Germany the Boys appeared on Viva, that country's version of MTV, singing and talking to fans, and the single went straight into the Top Ten, all the way to Number One. It was the same in Belgium and Holland.

Curiously, the European country that seemed to show the most initial resistance was England. The single did chart, but barely, only getting to #54—nowhere near as good as they'd hoped for, even if it did beat America.

The United States might not have immediately embraced their homies with open arms, but north of the border, in Canada, it was a different story altogether. Just like Germany, they took the Backstreet Boys to their hearts, and made "We've Got It Goin' On" into a major hit. Things might not be happening quite the way everyone around the band had planned, but things were very definitely happening!

Nick, Kevin, Brian, AJ, and Howie had to keep pinching themselves all through the end of 1995. This was way beyond even their wildest dreams. In Germany they did press, and girls would go crazy. Even in England, when they performed live all over the country, as the opening act on Ant And Dec's Christmas tour, fans were screaming, and the band was getting mobbed every night, the biggest hit of the entire show.

It was a time for some really big decisions. Should they concentrate on Europe, where they were doing incredibly well, and try to push themselves over the top there, or should they go home, keep trying to crack America, and capitalize on the success they were having in Canada?

Europe had to be the answer. Things were going *so* well there, that to walk away from it would have been stupid.

They'd already made their decision. But even if they hadn't, two events at the beginning of 1996 would have convinced them that Europe was the place for the Backstreet Boys right now.

In January, Take That announced their breakup. They'd been *the* biggest boy band ever in British musical history, with hit after hit after hit. They'd never managed to crack America, but given their success at home, it didn't really matter.

At the news, groups of girls literally gathered in the streets to cry and commiserate with each other. A hotline set up by the band and their management offered counseling.

But Take That's demise meant there was now a void among boy bands. East 17 was there, but they seemed to be trying to change their image and get a bit hipper.

But the Boys were there. They had the moves, they had the looks, and they could sing.

It was the second event that made it *really* seem as if they'd be the ones to take the crown vacated by Take That. In January the results of the annual poll held by pop magazine *Smash Hits* were announced, and readers had voted the Backstreet Boys Best Newcomers of the Year.

Considering they'd only released one single, and that hadn't been a big British hit, the response was incredible! And it was echoed by MTV Europe, who, after that and their mega-success on the European mainland, began calling the band the Kings of Pop!

The demands on their time were only just beginning. BSB were really starting to break, and if they thought they'd had to work before, well, now they were going to learn what it was all about. Their dance cards couldn't have been any more full.

The first thing was to go and satisfy fans in Canada, where the single had done so well. In particular, it had proved to be massive in Quebec, and so the Boys arranged a show in the province.

"We were really surprised the first time we went to Quebec and played at the [Place Vertu] mall in Montreal," says Kevin. "Over three thousand people showed up." It was the biggest crowd BSB had ever drawn, and they were blown away. But if he thought that was impressive, it was nothing compared to their return in six months later, in August. Then they performed at the Festival des Montgolsieres at St. Jean de Richelieu, just outside Montreal, and a staggering *65,000* came to see them!

After a short Canadian tour, it was back to Florida, but with no real time for a rest. The band hadn't completely given up on home. There was promotional work to be done, to keep the BSB name and Backstreet pride alive, hitting the radio stations, and letting the fans they did have know that they were still very much alive and kicking.

And there was another video to be made, too, this one for their next European (and Canadian) single, "Get Down (You're the One For Me)."

This was going to be an elaborate and very expensive production. The concept was odd, with the Boys in something resembling a dome, performing on a round stage, which was lit beneath, while the dome's walls were made of television screens, each containing girls' faces.

Not only did Kev, Nick, Brian, Howie, and AJ have to dance and sing, there was also plenty of time spent by each of them in front of a "blue screen." This process allowed their bodies to be superimposed anywhere on the set, giving the illusion of flying, and AJ, in particular, seemed to take off several times during the video!

"It was very interesting," Howie remembers, "because we were forced to use imagination. And it turned out really good."

The girls, too, would emerge from their TV sets and fly over the Boys on the stage.

Yes, it was all *very* strange, but that was exactly the point. It was the kind of video you saw and remembered: impressive, big budget, and you wanted to see it again and again just to try and figure the whole thing out. And the fact that the song had a totally insistent beat behind the sweet voices, and a killer chorus, wasn't going to hurt things one bit. This wasn't one of the songs they'd recorded in Stockholm, but in Florida.

"We had a lot of fun when we recorded it at Fun Factory!" says AJ. "I think it shows that we can rap a little bit, and it has more of that hip-hop sound."

And for Nick it was a favorite "because the choreography is great!"

Just because they were gone from Europe for a few weeks didn't mean that the Continent had forgotten about them. Particularly in England their star seemed to be rising, and while they were home filming the video, they won another British title, in the annual Red Nose Awards, where they were voted Best Newcomers!

As soon as the filming was complete, they were back on a plane for Germany. To coincide with the release of "Get Down (You're The One For Me)" they were set to embark on a gigantic thirty-five city tour.

By the time they hit the first stage, the single was already Number One, and it had entered charts all over the Continent. In Holland, Belgium, France, Spain, Italy, it had zapped into the Top Twenty. The Backstreet Boys had an appeal that crossed every kind of barrier, whether it was language or national borders.

For all their awards and popularity in England,

though, it only managed to crest at #14, better than the last record, but still a relatively poor showing in comparison to their continental cousins.

In Germany, though, it was complete Backstreet mania. Every show on the tour sold out in a matter of hours. The fans were just crazy for them. And these weren't just small shows—they were playing arenas that held several thousand people!

Fans would also follow them from the venue to their hotels and special events they were attending. On one occasion, their appearance at a radio station was announced in advance. By the time the Boys arrived, there was a massive crowd gathered outside the building. They managed to get inside, to talk to the DJ, and even perform a few songs a capella, as they always do live. But as soon as they opened the door to leave, it was total chaos.

"I mean, [the fans] were jammed in there and they had written 'Backstreet Boys' all over the walls," Howie recollects. "They would not move to save our lives. They all wanted to get ahold of us."

Even the Boys' security team couldn't get the fans to budge, and in the end BSB had no choice but to try and make a run for it. The problem was that everyone except AJ was wearing very distinctive jackets in red, white, and blue, emblazoned with "Backstreet Boys," making them easily stand out.

"They were pulling me and they were grabbing all over my jacket," Howie says. "I was grabbing for anything to hold onto my clothes."

The only one to escape unscathed was AJ, who'd chosen to wear a black jacket instead, and managed to get back to the van in one piece.

If that seemed crazy, when they appeared on Viva, things just got totally out of control.

"The mistake they made was publicizing all week that

the Backstreet Boys are going to be here,'' remembers AJ. "There were over two thousand girls waiting for us and they ended up walking and jumping on soft-top convertibles and putting holes in them. The ruckus they caused made Viva tell us they don't want us back."

It wasn't because they didn't like them—BSB were the hottest thing in Germany in years—but they just didn't want a repeat of the riot!

But those reactions were typical of the way they were received all over the country. Girls tried to sneak onto their tour bus, hiding in the luggage compartments or in the bathroom.

And at concerts it was even worse. The fans would climb any kind of obstacle to get closer to the Boys.

"One girl got caught up in [a barbed wire] fence," Nick remembers with astonishment, "and hung there by her pants. She ripped her bottoms off, climbed in a window in the venue and knocked on our dressing room door!"

There'd been nothing like it in a long, long time. Backstreet was just setting the country on fire. They were irresistible, and everyone who saw them in concert soon understood they were very much the real thing.

There were always two things that characterized a BSB show. One was that the Boys would take a lot of time to thank their fans. After all, they were the people who'd put them where they were now, who were shelling out money for their singles, their T-shirts, and to see them perform. It was something they couldn't—and didn't want to—forget. The fans had made them; they owed it all to them. All the talent in the world didn't matter if no one was paying attention.

The other thing was the a capella portion of their set, when they could bring stools onstage, and relax little, communicate with the fans. They were justifiably proud of the fact that they could sing, and sing very well. Having music behind them (the boys toured with a band of two keyboards, guitar, bass, and drums) was fine, but the real factor was their voices, and singing without accompaniment was what it was all about for them. It was how they'd started out, a little over three years before, and it would *always* be an important thing for them. They'd do a brief cover of the Boyz II Men favorite, "End of the Road," which had been a huge international smash, and Number One on the American charts for thirteen weeks in 1992, before going into "Just to be Close to You," a ballad they'd recorded for the album that would be coming later in the year, and one of Kevin's favorites because "I get to sing deep bass harmonies."

By the end of every show, they were totally drained. Each time they went on the stage, they gave it their all. But that was only fair—these were their fans they were performing for, and they deserved the best the Boys could possibly do.

The whole tour went very smoothly, although the constant routine of performing, hotel, traveling, and performing again was grueling. However, all the time they'd spent doing exactly that in America, long before they were really known, stood them in good stead. A lot of their day was boring, but they'd grown to accept that, and their hour in front of the crowds each night made everything worthwhile.

By the end of April, they were ready to fly home again. Not for a rest this time, however much they needed it. This was more business, to film two videos, for "Quit Playing Games (With My Heart)" and "I'll Never Break Your Heart," which had already been slated as the next two singles.

The "Quit Playing Games (With My Heart)" video was done very close to home, right in Orlando, on the outdoor basketball court at Howard Middle School. It was by far the sexiest they'd looked so far, with plenty of glimpses of the pecs and abs of the boys on the ballad.

A basketball court was the perfect place to find them,

really, given their love of the game. But it really had little to do with them playing. This was just pure romance on the screen, a plea to a girlfriend to be true— something they'd all experienced in real life, and could put their emotions into.

"I'll Never Break Your Heart" took them from the warmth of Florida up into the mountains, a chance to try their hands at skiing and sledding. While it was one of the most sincere songs they'd ever recorded, the video was playful, having them falling down a lot, trying to do all the snow sports with a group of girls.

There was no break for the successful. The long days of shooting finished, they were back on a plane and bound for Heathrow, in London. "Get Down (You're The One for Me)" was still on the British charts, and the Boys wanted to bolster its success, and say thank you to their very supportive fans there, by appearing on *Top of the Pops,* the weekly chart show, and also on a children's show, *Fully Booked.*

Then it was back on the road, playing more dates in England, and all across Europe, during June and July, stirring up audiences and causing pandemonium wherever they went.

The beginning of August found them back in England. "We've Got It Goin' On," which hadn't exactly been a smash in Britain the first time around, was being re-released. The whole affair was celebrated with a party at a very trendy club, The Emporium, and this time the record literally exploded out of the box, going straight into the Top Ten the first week it was out, and rising all the way to #3, just to cement BSB's position as the top boy band in Europe.

Here's where it gets really confusing: In different countries, the band released different singles. "We've Got It Goin' On" had been the first one *everywhere*, but after that it all changed. Britain got "Get Down (You're the

One for Me)'' then the reissue of "We've Got It Goin' On.''

Meanwhile, in the rest of Europe, where the first single had gone mega, it was followed by "Get Down (You're The One for Me),'' and then "I'll Never Break Your Heart,'' the video for which the Boys had just filmed. That, of course, was another smash, but there was no way the Boys could get over to see their fans for this one. By the time it came out, they were in Canada, playing to the biggest audiences of their career all across the country. By anyone's standards, a crowd of 65,000 is a lot of people, but that was the number of fans who turned out in Montreal. And as they headed west, the numbers stayed big. They'd had two huge singles there, and now "I'll Never Break Your Heart'' was topping the Canadian charts, just as it was all over Europe.

It seemed as if everywhere they went, except for America, the Boys could do absolutely no wrong. But there was one area they hadn't turned their attention to yet, and that was next on the agenda—Asia.

What's successful in Europe is picked up quite quickly in Asia, and the Backstreet Boys were the kind of band it was impossible to resist. They looked great, and sounded even better, the perfect combination. "We've Got It Goin' On" and "I'll Never Break Your Heart" had both been released, and had been hits from Singapore to Australia, but not the absolute smashes they'd become.

The world really needed a Backstreet Boys album, and it would be coming very, very soon. But first the Boys needed a little time to wind down. Things had seemed pretty amazing before, but once the album hit the streets all over the world—except America—things were going to get *really* wild!

"It was weird," Nick recalls, "because we'd play shows to, like, ten thousand fans in Europe, then we'd come back home and walk down the street and no one would recognize us. It was a humbling experience, because now we want to show everybody, 'Look, this is what we've been doing.' "

But America wasn't going to have a chance to be shown for quite a long time yet. That was one area the album definitely wouldn't be released, not until the band could really focus their energies on the country, and have it join everywhere else as Backstreet turf.

The album, *Backstreet Boys* was released in the fall

of 1996, September in Asia, mid-October in Europe and Canada.

Depending on where you lived, there were two different versions of *Backstreet Boys*. In Canada it had ten tracks, but in Europe and Asia, there were fourteen tracks! And that wasn't all—the European version included two bonus cuts, tracks recorded live in Europe during the Boys' tours.

Every edition of the album had ''We've Got It Goin' On,'' ''Get Down (You're The One For Me),'' ''I'll Never Break Your Heart,'' ''Quit Playing Games (With My Heart),'' ''Boys Will Be Boys,'' ''Just To Be Close To You,'' ''I Wanna Be with You,'' ''Every Time I Close My Eyes,'' ''Darlin','' and ''Roll With It.''

In Europe and Asia the fans were also treated to ''Anywhere For You,'' ''Let's Have A Party'' (which they always used to open their shows), ''Nobody But You,'' and ''Don't Leave Me.''

All very complicated, but no more so than the order in which singles had been released and re-released in different countries. And even if it made no sense, it really didn't matter. Any way you looked at it, whether you got ten tracks or a total of sixteen, it was all great music.

Some songs were already familiar through the hit singles, but there was plenty of new material, all of which was guaranteed to please. ''Just To Be Close To You'' bore no resemblance to the old Carpenters' song, but was instead what Brian called their ''percapella song''—just voices and a drum track. ''I Wanna Be With You'' rocked the house, with a hard, exciting riff, AJ in the lead giving it a very street, almost hip-hop feel. ''Every Time I Close My Eyes'' caught a groove, the perfect type of slow jam for five voices to work their magic. ''Let's Have A Party'' was pure happiness, the kind of thing to make you want to move the furniture and get ready to have a good time. ''Roll With It'' was definitely *not* the Oasis song of the same name. In Britain it had been the B-side of "I'll Never Break Your Heart," one of four songs that Brian, Kev, Howie, Nick, and AJ had recorded over the course of a week, but one they really liked. It was a real message song, since at times everyone feels alone, as if nobody else cares. The Boys were saying that if you just hung in there a little longer, things really would get better.

"Nobody But You" took them into slightly different territory, as AJ explained. "When you hear it you can imagine it being in a movie soundtrack, it's got that vibe. It's got a Seventies sound, with jazzy, funky guitars." With Kevin taking the lead in the dark brown velvet voice, it worked perfectly.

The closer, "Don't Leave Me," could almost have been an ad for Florida, it contained so much sunshine, the ideal, happy way to end a great record, even if many of the tracks would never be heard in their home country. But everywhere else appreciated it. Even before it was released, *Backstreet Boys* was a massive international hit, simply from the advance orders.

To coincide with the album, "Anywhere For You" was issued as a single throughout Asia, and went straight into the Top Ten as BSB did a promotional tour at the beginning of October, moving like a whirlwind through Singapore, Malaysia, Korea, and the Philippines—areas a lot of Western artists didn't bother to visit. In addition, a month later, "I'll Never Break Your Heart" was reissued, and became a hit for the second time, on this occasion climbing much higher up the charts, all the way to Number One, giving the Boys two records nestling together at the top of the singles chart, while the album simply flew out of stores, going platinum in a matter of weeks.

But the demand for *Backstreet Boys* was huge all over the world. In Germany, to no one's surprise and everyone's delight, it went straight to Number One. In Britain it entered the album charts at #12, and rising. And in Canada it was a platinum record within days of its release—the first country where it went platinum, in fact, although plenty of others would soon join it in acclaiming the Boys as the biggest boy band around—by far.

From Asia, it was back to Europe for the Boys, to do promotion for *Backstreet Boys.* That meant record signings, public appearances, a chance for the fans to get close to them. At times, though, that seemed to get out of control. A signing at a record store in Germany drew scarily large crowds, and brought on a riot.

"We signed CDs for five minutes," is how Brian remembers it, "We had a chance to sign maybe ten autographs—and the girls busted through the barriers. They wrecked the store and stole posters and stand-ups of us that they had on display."

In London, with a break between commitments, AJ and Howie tried to spend a touristy evening around Picadilly Circus, just catching some sights, getting a bite to eat, and meeting some friends. It was supposed to be relaxed, low-key, and so they'd come out of the hotel without any security. That seemed like a good idea until fans spotted them and cornered them. An hour later the pair were still signing autographs. ". . . [W]e were like, 'Okay, okay, okay,' and we're trying to work our way back into the mall area," AJ remembers.

Maybe their lives were becoming a little restricted, but at the same time, everything they were touching was turning to gold—or platinum. Even triple platinum in Canada, as well as Singapore, Hong Kong, Indonesia, and Germany. In the Philippines, it was a staggering sextuple (6x) platinum!

Before long, the album had gone gold or platinum in an amazing thirty-five countries! That put the Boys up there in some very rarified air, as one of the world's best-selling acts, and it would sell some ten million copies.

*   *   *

For now, though, they had to think about being back onstage, as it was time to undertake another European tour, as "I'll Never Break Your Heart" was released there, and banged into Top Tens everywhere. Of course, all the shows were sold out well in advance, and *Vidz* magazine named them as Best Band. But the biggest thrill came not from the performances themselves, but from something that took place on television.

On November 3 and 4, 1996, MTV Europe held a special Select MTV weekend. It was a nine-hour marathon in which the top 100 videos were aired. Viewers could call in and name their favorite bands, and the top five would be the nominees for the Select MTV Award—with the ultimate winner to again be decided by viewers. The band was astonished and flattered when they were named as one of the nominees, but nowhere near as happy as they would be a month later. There, at the MTV Europe Awards, held in Alexandra Palace, London, they stepped onto the stage to receive the Select MTV Award, easily beating out the competition, which included the Spice Girls.

And giving it to them was Robbie Williams, who'd once been the leader of Take That, the biggest boy band ever in Europe—until Backstreet. It was as if the crown was being passed, and the Backstreet Boys really were the new Kings of Pop.

In 1996, beating the Spice Girls was quite an achievement. Although the Girls only had records out for six months, their first single "Wannabe" had gone to the top of the charts in a staggering thirty-seven countries around the globe, and it's follow-ups, "Say You'll Be There" and "2 Becomes 1" had also been international smashes. They were the first girl group to be completely in-your-face about things, as laddish as any lads. They'd rocketed out of nowhere to become stars, the Queens of Pop.

Between Spice and Backstreet, it all seemed to herald a great new age for pop music. This was what people were buying, it was what they really, really wanted to listen to. The days of alienation, of grunge and alternative all over the charts, seemed to be on the wane. Even in rock music, it was Oasis who were calling the shots, playing songs with choruses and melodies that seemed to hark back to the pop music of the Sixties, albeit with a Nineties edge.

1996 had been an incredible year for the Boys. They'd not only broken through, but they'd done it in such style that they'd become global megastars. About the only place they could walk down the street without being mobbed was in their homeland, which was ironic, really, but would all be taken care of in due course.

To celebrate their MTV Award, and to see the year out in fine style, they toured Europe again, selling out shows in minutes all across the Continent. In Germany the 10,000-seat halls were hardly big enough to accommodate their fans.

One of the concerts from that tour, at the Festhalle, in Frankfurt, was broadcast live on Premiere TV, an hour of the Boys singing and entertaining. It was a chance for everyone who couldn't get tickets to see all the facets that AJ, Howie, Nick, Brian, and Kevin had to display.

It all began with the video screens above the stage lighting up. As each of the guys was announced, there'd be pictures of them as babies, then boys, then teens, to the way they were now. After the buildup was complete, they exploded onto the stage to open with "Let's Have a Party," with AJ, in particular, looking extremely cool in a new goatee and long, thin sideburns, his hair dark again after several months as a blond. They danced, moved, and got the crowd completely on their side, and then they took it all the way down, sitting on stools and crooned a capella on "End Of The road" and "Just To

Be Close To You,'' before starting to build again with
''I'll Never Break Your Heart.'' Kevin went into the
crowd during ''Anywhere For You.'' This was a song
with special resonance for the Boys. While it was a love
song, they saw it as a message that they really would go
anywhere and do almost anything for their fans, and Kev
proved it, taking his life and safety into his hands as he
went to shake hands with the front rows, while people
grabbed for him and tried to rip his clothes off. Most of
the songs were already familiar to the audience from the
Backstreet Boys, but there were a couple of oddities in
there—the instrumental ''Ain't Nobody,'' played by the
band (two keyboards, guitar, bass, and drums) while the
Boys did a quick costume change, and ''10,000 Promises,'' which *hadn't* appeared on the record, and
wouldn't actually see the light of day until *Backstreet's
Back* was released in the fall of 1997.

Over and over they thanked the crowd, in both English and German, for their support, and even involved
them in the singing, splitting them into two halves to
join in on different lines of the chorus for ''Darlin'.''

After that came the lights went down, and suddenly a
drum set rose out of the floor at the front of the stage.
Nick came out of the darkness, and began to play, walking around the kit to do his solo. Then Kevin joined him,
and, presto, a piano was there for him, as they dueted
on ''10,000 Promises,'' Kevin singing solo and playing,
while Nick kept the solid beat behind him. It was a
chance for them both to show their instrumental skills,
which were far more than just basic, and have a few
minutes basking in the spotlight. Once it was over,
Kevin asked the crew to turn on the halls lights so he
could videotape the audience, *''fur meine familie.''*

After that it was into the big finale, all five of them
onstage for slammin' versions of ''Boys Will Be Boys''
and ''Get Down (You're The One For Me).'' The lights
came up, it was all over . . . except for the fact the fans

wouldn't stop shouting and clapping. So an encore was definitely in order, and it was an extended version of "Quit Playing Games (With My Heart)," the perfect closer, since it would be their next Number One single.

It was a great Backstreet experience, but typical of the way every concert went, the audience totally mad for them, and the guys happy to give it their all in return, to show their gratitude. A few months later the show would be released as a home video, "Backstreet Boys Live In Concert" all over the world, a treat for fans who hadn't seen them in a while, or had just recently discovered their music.

Not every show went quite as smoothly as the televised concert from Festhalle. On the last night of that tour (and last nights have always been ones for lots of tricks, particularly around the Boys, who love to play them, Nick being the worst of them all) it was absolute craziness, and the turn of the road crew to enjoy some fun at the Boys' expense.

"Our crew was trying stuff with us," AJ says, recalling the practical joke that was played. "We did the song 'Boys Will Be Boys' where we're supposed to dance with our mikestands. They put carrots on our mikestands! I didn't know what it was and I couldn't stop laughing!"

It was all in good fun, and in just a few seconds the microphones were in place and the show continued.

The Backstreet Boys also had one other treat for fans, just to round the year off to perfection. Along with their concert schedule, they managed to fit in a little television, including appearances on some charity shows, and it was there they previewed something they'd recorded as a thank you to their audiences all over for making this year so incredibly memorable, a song called "Christmas Time," which was distributed only to members of the BSB fan club.

1996 had ended with a bang louder than any bomb. It seemed like they'd done it all—hit records, sold-out shows, adoring fans. The question was, of course, how could they top all that in '97?

♪ 1997 ♪

The answer to that question came in the form of a new single, "Quit Playing Games (With My Heart)," which was released in January 1997, and proved to be their biggest hit so far, keeping the Backstreet pride very much alive. This was the one that cemented their status as a major group of the decade, a true pop force of nature. It entered the British Top Ten at #4, rising to #2, and those kinds of positions (in fact, in many countries it went directly to Number One) were repeated everywhere, a monumental smash hit. They were back in the UK, playing some more shows, and receiving the *Smash Hits* Award for Best Road Show, before heading on to Canada for a series of dates there that would culminate on the West Coast. Like Germany, Canada had been one of the first countries to embrace BSB. The album had gone triple platinum in a matter of weeks, and now it was 9x platinum, a standard hardly anyone had ever reached before.

No matter where their concerts were scheduled, every ticket was snapped up as soon as they went on sale. Europe, Canada . . . about the only area they hadn't played where they were huge was Asia, where *Backstreet Boys* had sold 1.3 million copies! By American standards that might not seem much, but in Asia it was incredible!

In February, Europe got even more BSB, as "Anywhere For You'' was released as a single, just in time for Valentine's Day; there was even a limited-edition Valentine's version of the record, with special messages from each of the Boys—pretty close to the perfect gift for any Backstreet fan. By now it was a given that anything they released was going to be big, and this joined "Quit Playing Games (With My Heart)'' in the upper reaches of charts around the world for several weeks.

Although there seemed to be no shortage of hits, and *Backstreet Boys* was still doing the business in every country where it could be bought, it was already time for the Boys to be thinking ahead to their next album. After all, it was almost two years since they'd recorded most of the tracks for their debut, and they'd come a long way since then. In many ways they'd grown up on the road, and that was particulay true for AJ and Nick, who were, respectively, nineteen and seventeen now, not at all the kids they'd been at the beginning of Backstreet. Everyone had learned a lot, about music, about each other, and about the world. They were more mature now, and becoming stars had made them grow up fast. It was a great life, but it also had its responsibilities, which they all acknowledged and accepted; that helped them keep themselves grounded, as Nick explains. "It's been quite an adjustment,'' he admits. "But we have good family support and that helps us keep our heads on our shoulders and our feet on the ground.''

The Boys took time to begin picking out material for a new record, and soon had the list narrowed down. Once again there'd be songs from Sweden, from Denniz PoP and Max Martin, and Timmy Allen, who'd co-written "Darlin' '' on *Backstreet Boys,* had brought in "Hey Mr. DJ (Keep Playin' This Song)'' along with two new writing partners. But the biggest thrill of all when when a song one of the Boys had written made the cut for the album.

They all wrote, and in time they aspired to write and produce a whole album for themselves. But, they realized, that was in the future. But "That's What She Said," B-Rok's composition, was a first small step toward that goal, and a pretty amazing achievement in itself. That he'd even had the time to write a song in the last year was remarkable, given the whirlwind life the boys had been living. That it turned out to be so good was a testament to a whole lot of natural talent.

Before they began any recording, though, the Boys really needed a vacation. 1996 might have just sped by, but during that time they'd logged an awful lot of miles, sung in so many different places, and seen so many faces. They were exhausted. Everything had been nonstop, and they needed someplace they could just chill, where there'd be no fans, just sea and sand and sun, a chance for them to wind down properly and be refreshed.

Florida was one possibility, but that was home. What they *really* wanted was a vacation, and there was only one destination that completely fit the bill—Hawaii.

Kevin took his best bud, Trey D., with whom he'd moved from Lexington to Orlando. Nick brought along his mom, Jane, as well as sister BJ and little brother Aaron, while AJ's mother, Jane, came along, as usual, to be the chaperone.

It was eight days on Maui, staying in the Maui Marriott, right on the beach.

"During the first two days we just spent our time suntanning," Brian told *Bravo*, "but now we need some action. We have been swimming, surfing, and playing many different sports."

There was certainly plenty to keep them busy, and something they all discovered, and loved, were the Boogie boards, which they used in the surf.

By the third day Kevin was nursing a bad sunburn on his neck. He might have been used to the Florida sun, but a year of hotels and buses had taken away his tan base—something he'd forgotten when he went into the sun! The others were more cautious, limiting their exposure, and spending a lot more time in the shade.

It was a time to unveil a new-look BSB, too. Kevin had cut his hair short, but AJ had gone one better—shaving his off completely. "It's very practical when you go swimming," he explained. They weren't the only two to make some changes. B-Rok had not only grown his sideburns, he'd also dyed his hair red!

By the third day they were really feeling relaxed and good, and ready for some real Hawaiian hospitality, which took place in the evening, with a traditional luau.

"We had so much fun," Howie told the magazine, "me and the guys sang a few songs with the ukulele to Aaron!"

A pair of hula dancers, Laui and Tempa, put on a show for them, the real deal with the grass skirts, and the Boys attempted to join in. Amazingly, though, considering how athletic and coordinated they were onstage, according to Brian, "we couldn't do the hula dance well!"

The remaining five days were quieter, as the Boys *really* took advantage of the opportunity to relax, knowing that their year was already entirely booked. More than a year, in fact, pretty much until the middle of 1998. There was going to be a long, long stretch in front of them, one without any real breaks, and they needed to be completely rested before any of that.

It was a definite time to chill, to soak up some rays, to smell the sea air and try to think about nothing, although after the year they'd had thinking about nothing must have been close to impossible.

But all too soon it was time to put their leis aside and board a plane to take them back to Orlando, and begin work on their new album, which, it was decided, would be called *Backstreet's Back*. A lot of the recording would take place at a studio they'd become familiar with when laying down the vocals for *Backstreet Boys*—Parc Studios, right at home in Orlando. But there'd also be some traveling, to New York, where some of the tracks would be recorded at Battery Studios and The Hit Factory, and a side trip to Philadelphia, for "Fitz" Gerald Scott's composition, "Like A Child," which would team the Boys up with an orchestra. This would be done at Sigma Studios, the home of the famous Philadelphia Sound of Gamble and Huff which had produced a lot of hits in the 1970s for the O'Jays and other soul groups.

This time Denniz PoP was traveling from Sweden to record them on their home turf; by now BSB were big enough that most producers came to *them*, not the other way round. Even Robert John "Mutt" Lange was doing that. He was producing one track, "If You Want It To Be Good Girl (Get Yourself A Bad Boy)," which he'd also written. Mutt Lange had made his name as a producer back in the Seventies, and kept it alive all through the Eighties, working with a number of very big-name rock acts, ranging from Queen to AC/DC, and totally finding the mark with Def Leppard. But in the Nineties he'd moved more toward country, working with his wife, one of the biggest new names in modern country, Canada's Shania Twain. So, well known as he was, for him to work with someone like BSB was a step away from the norm.

It was, like everything Backstreet, absolute madness. They were in such demand that they could have cloned themselves and still been busy twenty-four hours a day. And so everything about the record had to be very carefully organized.

"We would go for two or three different sessions at a time in the studio," Howie recalls, "then split up the work. Some of us would be doing background, others would be doings the songs."

Brian's song, "That's What She Said," was, of course, recorded in Orlando, and Brian even took a hand in the production, along with Mookie, who, with Brian, Lenny Mollings, and Tommy Smith, also helped arrange the song, while the Boys contributed heavily to the vocal arrangement.

Maybe the biggest surprise among the tracks was the fact that they'd be covering "Set Adrift On Memory Bliss," which had been a Number One hit for P.M. Dawn at the end of 1991. Back then it had incorporated a lot of Spandau Ballet's Eighties hit, "True," as Prince Be, explains: "I basically reincarnated the spirit of 'True' for me. I reshaped it as if I wrote it myself, creating 'Set Adrift on Memory Bliss.' "

Of course there was full credit to Gary Kemp, who'd written "True." But the Boys took the song one stage further, using a sample from "How High," the hip-hop tune that had paired Redman and Wu Tang Clan's Method Man as part of their version.

"Like A Child" wasn't the only song on *Backstreet's Back* to bring in strings, either. This time around, the Boys had the time and the money to give everything a special polish, and that meant using real strings on the ballads, as opposed to synthesizers and samples. They also featured heavily in the accompaniment to Brian's "That's What She Said" and "If I Don't Have You." This was going to be a record that went for the gold, in every possible way. *Backstreet Boys* had made them stars, and now they were ready to take the leap to superstardom, which meant that everything had to be just right, a state of affairs that particularly suited Kevin, the perfectionist in the group.

There was one song they'd recorded that didn't make it onto the album, however. Kenneth Edmonds, better known to the world as Babyface, a writer and producer of any number of hits for people like Toni Braxton and Eric Clapton, not to mention himself, had contributed a song, and the Boys had sung it. According to Kevin, however, "He didn't have time to produce it so we used someone else. We didn't like the results we got, so we're waiting until he has the time to do it himself before including it on an album.'' And that was something to look forward to, for everyone—BSB *and* fans.

It would be several months before *Backstreet's Back* would make its way to the fans, however. That was okay, because there was still plenty to keep the guys out of too much mischief.

To begin, it was back on the road, a place they knew very well these days, with another tour, and then the preparations for what would be their chance to dominate the world—finally conquering America.

It was something they'd always wanted, to be acknowledged in their own country, and who could blame them? Even now, they could walk down the street in Orlando, go to the mall or the 7-11 and the only fans who'd speak to them were those who'd traveled from abroad.

It was an odd situation, but if they had any say in the matter, all that would change.

''We're definitely ready for success at home,'' Howie said at the time. ''We're ready to bring it home.''

It wasn't just a case of success for its own sake; they also had something to prove, as Kevin pointed out.

''We want our teachers, friends, and family to see what we've done with our lives.''

Really, according to Barry Weiss, the president of Jive Records, the Boys' label, everyone had been very patient.

''We said to ourselves, waiting is better, firstly because the more international information and word-of-mouth we can build on the group, the more ammunition we have in America, and secondly because we'd been hitting the teen fanzines, doing 1-800 numbers and all those things for two years without a record being out.''

And there was that core of fans they'd made when touring the high schools in 1993 and '94. Granted, they were a little older now, and many of them would have different tastes. But some would still remember BSB very kindly. And some of the freshmen would still be in school.

Of course, they knew there'd be problems, and possibly some resistance. A few people would, ironically, think they were English, since they'd had so much success over there. Also, there were a lot of people who didn't remember New Kids On The Block too kindly, and would inevitably compare the Boys to them.

While it was true that both bands had fans among teens, the two weren't the same.

"With New Kids On The Block and Take That, most of their fan base was the young teen market," Kevin pointed out in *Billboard*, "so as soon as you see another bunch of guys, you stereotype them or put them in the same cateogry ... success made us more well rounded. It changed our perspectives on the way the world is."

Could they break America? The answer would come in July, when the "Quit Playing Games (With My Heart)" single reached the stores, and the video began to appear on MTV.

Before that, there was so much to do that for the guys to focus on America was impossible until the time came. Their tour culminated with a show at England's Wembley Arena, in London, for well over 13,000 fans on June 26, after more dates in Germany and Austria.

As shows went, this was the biggest they'd played in Britain, the pinnacle, and it meant that they'd made it as a massive band—only the biggest acts ever managed to sell out the Arena. Some fans had been waiting outside for twenty-four hours by the time the doors opened, just to be able to get close to the Boys. It didn't matter that they had to spend hours waiting in an English summer rain—this was worth every minute.

Among the opening acts was Nick's little brother,

Aaron, who received great support from the crowd. He'd been with the band in Germany, and already had a single out in Europe, which had been doing well, with an entire CD of material planned for later in the year.

But even he couldn't compete with the real thing.

This was a slightly different show from their last tour. There were still the pictures of each of the guys to introduce them, but the material was moved around a little, with plenty of new songs thrown into the mix. They opened with "We Got It Goin' On," then went into "Let's Have A Party." There was no Boys II Men cover this time time around, only "Just To Be Close To You" in the a capella section, before a preview of the storming new single, "Everybody (Backstreet's Back)," followed by "I'll Never Break Your Heart."

Then it was time for each of the Boys to have a solo showcase. Kevin came on first to sing "Nobody But You." When he was done, Howie appeared and covered the old hit (recently revived by one of his favorites, Prince), "Betcha By Golly Wow," where he could let his falsetto glide over the lines. Nick did "Heaven," and then Brian used a set of a bookcase, table, and chair to sit and croon "One Last Cry." Last up was AJ, but he finished the solo section on a very high note indeed, reviving the Commodores' disco classic, "Brick House" to get all of Wembley dancing along.

After that all five of the Boys were back onstage together, running through "I Wanna Be With you," "Anywhere For You," and "Darlin'," still staples of their live set.

Then, as they had on previous tours, Nick got his drum solo, and Kevin came and duetted on "10,000 Promises" with him, before the finale of "Boys Will Be Boys" followed by "Get Down (You're The One For Me)."

That they'd escape without an encore was unthinkable, as 13,000 people shook the floor and the walls, demanding more, more, more. And they got it, in the form of "Quit Playing Games (With My Heart)."

It was a show in transition. The new album wasn't out yet, but once it was, BSB would be including more material from it. and that new record was on their minds as soon as they emerged, showered and changed, from the dressing room, went to Heathrow, and boarded a flight to Los Angeles, where they were going to shoot three videos for their next three singles.

"When we were in LA," AJ recounts, "we met Quad City DJs, Dru Hill, Joe, Blackstreet, Salt 'n' Pepa, LL Cool J . . . all staying in our hotel, shooting videos! It must have been 'shoot your video in LA' week."

The shoots themselves were always long and laborious, involving take after take of every scene from different angles. But even longer, and more tedious, was the preparation, since every one involved choreography that had to be worked out, practiced, and perfected—hours and hours of work. Then there were the costumes and the makeup, and all manner of things.

"As Long As You Love Me" and "All I Have To Give" were both done with British director Nigel Dicks. The first was pure fun, the Boys auditioning for a group of female executives, being filmed, and showing the geeky side of their personalities (the best being AJ on a chair with a steering wheel, pretending to drive (pretty good for someone who'd only managed to get his license a year before!), and Kev as a surfer, before they turned the tables, and saw the "inner girls" playing around. There was also a very cool dance with chairs, where, thanks to the miracles of editing, each of the guys turned into another member of the band.

"All I Have To Give" was a little more straightforward, with lots of moody shots and heavy shadows, but also the Boys dancing, dressed in shiny silver suits.

The biggie, though, was the video for "Everybody (Backstreet's Back)," which would be the first single off the album. It was more than just a video, but a short film, a Nineties version of Michael Jackson's "Thriller" (although not as long; "Thriller" runs almost thirty minutes). That made sense. Most of the band had grown up watching MTV, and "Thriller" had, without any doubt, been *the* video, as well as one of the major songs, of the Eighties, a formative time for them all.

The idea for the video had come from the band themselves, sparking when they were on an airplane, and for all of them it was remarkable to see it taking shape in front of their eyes. Working with a young director, Joseph Kahn (who'd also done videos for Shaquille O'Neal in the past, and who was very used to working with speical effects), the concept was fleshed out.

On tour, the Boys' bus breaks down, forcing them to take shelter in an old castle. Asleep, each of the guys dreams, and becomes a character out of horror literature, culminating in a huge dance scene in the castle's ballroom. The next morning they compare dreams, and leave, only to be confronted with a bus driver who's gone crazy!

Each of the guys got to pick his own character. For Howie D, the Latin lover, it was pretty obvious—Count Dracula. Brian made a very natural werewolf, one with a very Seventies style, AJ was the Phantom of the Opera, Nick a Mummy, while Kevin got to show both sides of his personality by being Dr. Jekyll and Mr. Hyde.

The sets were put together in a disused airplane hangar, about the only place big enough for everything, and as carpenters and painters got to work, the Boys and the rest of the cast were busy in the studio, working with their choreographer to get everything right for the big dance scene.

The filming itself was squeezed into three very long days, although, as Kahn himself pointed out, two weeks would have been a lot better. But three days was all the Boys could manage in their hectic schedule, and they were the ones who had to be up at five every morning to go into makeup and hair.

Nick's makeup took less than anyone else's, and that still lasted four hours. Poor Kev was in there for six hours! While one was getting ready, another was shooting his individual scenes, almost like a production line.

All made up, they couldn't even eat, and could only drink through straws. As photographer Andre Csillas, who was there the whole time, remembers, "The one with the worst costume was probably Brian. With his false teeth, he couldn't even speak! Howie had quite the same problem with his Dracula's teeth. No, it wasn't lots of fun for them."

Each day of the shoot lasted fourteen hours for Backstreet, and they came into it having just finished the taping of the "All I Have to Give" video the day before; in fact, while they'd been working on that, they'd also been rehearsing for "Everybody (Backstreet's Back)." If anyone ever thought stardom was all glamour and no work, they needed to take a look at the Boys in full swing.

Of course, if everything had gone perfectly, it would have been too easy. There had to be several glitches. Nick's sequence required three hours of non-stop work, with his make up adjusted every few sceonds, whenever he moved. That evening, when Kahn saw the rushes, he realized there'd been a problem with the film, and it all had to be reshot!

Nor did Kevin escape lightly. His sequence required him to have live rats running over his head and shoulders! Luckily, that didn't bother him too much—until the rats decided they wanted to be someplace warmer and decided to burrow under his clothes.

"I could see in Kevin's eyes what was happening in his head," remembers Csillas. "He was thinking, 'Either I burst out laughing and we have to start everything again, [or] I continue.' Well, he continued!"

The climax, the ballroom scene, involved some thirty dancers performing some very intricate, coordinated moves; luckily, all that came off without any mishaps, and finally the Boys were all done. Then it was on a plane again, and off to Dallas, Texas, for their first American show in almost three years, appearing on a bill with one of Howie's heros, Jon Secada, as well as Erasure and Blondie.

It was time for the big American push to begin.

♪ 1997—AMERICA ♪

There was no doubt what the single would be, but as to the album that would accompany it, that was altogether a different matter. Should they just issue *Backstreet Boys,* and if so, which version? The Canadian, or the one that had appeared in the rest of the world? Or perhaps they should skip that altogether, and have America be like everywhere else and ride the *Backstreet's Back* wave (although that, too, would be in different versions, depending on where you lived).

The answer seemed to lie in the best of both worlds. Their first U.S. album would be called *Backstreet Boys,* but it would be nothing like their debut elsewhere in the world. Even the cover would be different—the same shot, in fact, that would grace *Backstreet's Back* around the globe. And in terms of tracks, it would be more or less a compilation, a best of those first two albums. Six of the tracks would come from the *real Backstreet Boys* album (non-Canadian)—"We've Got It Goin' On," "Quit Playing Games (With My heart)"—of course, since it was the single, "Get Down (You're The One For Me)," "Anywhere For You," "I'll Never Break Your Heart," and "Darlin'," with the remaining six coming from *Backstreet's Back.* More than that, it would be an enhanced CD, so that people with computers and CD-ROM drives would be able to see as well as hear the Boys, and get an idea of who they really were. There were brief interviews with each member, all five of them, clips from some of the videos, and even a teaser of them in concert. It was a smart move, one which would help win them a lot of friends across the country, more effective than any article could ever be, seen by so many of the people who bought the record.

All in all, *Backstreet Boys* made the perfect primer, with all the big worldwide singles included, a real powerhouse record. All it had to do was sell.

This time around, though, America seemed very open to the Backstreet Boys.

"I think the market is more ready for a group like us now," Howie D said in an interview. "I think at the time we released our first record, alternative, grunge, and urban were hot. Now we feel that pop music is starting to come back a little bit."

It was a good assessment. The year 1997 had seen the return of real pop bands, ones whose big appeal was to the traditional pop market—teenagers. Both the Spice Girls and Hanson had been huge during the year, effectively priming the pump for the return of BSB in full effect.

From the day it was released, "Quit Playing Games (With My Heart)" had American hit written all over it. The Boys were all committed to promoting both it and the album before they had to return to Europe, and they went all out to make their success very real at home. Still, as AJ said at the time, "You really don't know what to expect."

One thing they probably hadn't anticipated was the way fans would react. In Europe and Canada they were used to crowds turning out to see them. Home, though, had always been different. So when they arrived at Tower Records in Torrance, California, for an autograph session, they were amazed to see several hundred screaming girls waiting for them. It was Germany all over again, if on a slightly smaller scale.

The attention was a sure sign that things were really beginning to happen for Backstreet in the U.S. An even surer sign was when the single entered the *Billboard* Hot 100 and began climbing, although everyone was holding their breath, hoping it would go higher than #69 (where "We've Got It Goin' On" had stalled two years before). There was no cause for alarm, as it entered at an amazing #24, they could all begin to relax—and begin rehearsals for their new tour, which would be massive, starting with outdoor festivals in Germany during August and September, and lasting well into the summer of 1998.

Everything would be revamped, bringing in a lot of material from *Backstreet's Back,* and also having a completely new stage set, which, AJ said, was "gonna be like kind of a Medieval set-up, but also half the stage is done up like the *Enterprise* off 'Star Trek'—superhuman, futuristic type stuff."

And there was also the (virtually) worldwide release of "Everybody (Backstreet's Back)" in July to consider, which meant that the boys made a high-speed tour all around the globe to promote it and introduce that very expensive new video. They might have been worried that fans would have forgotten them while they'd been away recording and concentrating on America, but they needn't have done. On the first week of its release, it debuted in the Top Ten in ten different countries—Austria, Canada, Britain, Germany, Switzerland, Holland, Italy, the Philippines, Hong Kong, and Spain—in the last two it had gone straight in at Number One! The video went directly into heavy rotation on Much Music, YTV, and Musique Plus in Canada, Viva in Germany, TMF in Holland, and MTV all across Europe and Asia.

At the start of August, though, just as everyone was gearing up for the release of *Backstreet's Back* later in the month, there was a very worrying piece of news. The Boys had been scheduled to fly to Ibiza, to tape a special for German television. Suddenly that was cancelled, as it was announced that Nick was suffering from clinical exhaustion, having collapsed during a BSB rehearsal.

"I didn't collapse," he told reporters. "It was just too hot in the hall and I felt a bit ill. I went to the doctor and he told me to rest, but I'm fine now."

Even so, the cancellation seemed justified. In two years of incredibly hard work, the Boys had enjoyed less than a month of real vacation, and their schedules were such that they were busy for a good twelve hours of every day—the type of thing no one could keep up for too long.

But they still had plenty ahead of them, and right now their next stop was Germany, followed by Austria and Switzerland to play their first stadium dates, all outdoors, thirteen sold-out concerts—sold out *way* in advance, as soon as the tickets went on sale—to a total of 360,000 fans. It was the ideal way to celebrate a new hit album, which had already gone platinum in several countries. BSB had become a totally unstoppable force.

This was the first real chance to try out all the new special effects, and the first date, in Hannover, was the real test. Everything had gone smoothly in rehearsal, but how would it all work live?

For the most part, the answer was fine, except for two chandeliers above the band. At the end of the show, they were supposed to go up in flames, and they did, but the guys all got a little worried as the liquid used for the fire began dripping on them. But no accidents happened. And before the concert's climax, "Get Down (You're The One For Me)" they were supposed to disappear from the stage, and quickly reappear somewhere else— pure illusion, of course, which involved crawling *under* the stage to reach the new location. As they came up, giant sparklers lit up, and for a second AJ thought he was on fire.

One stop on the tour, though, didn't involve any singing, but a chance to do something they all loved—play basketball.

It was their game of choice, and they took a collapsible hoop on the road with them that could be set up in venues and give them a chance to play and exercise at soundchecks. This, though, would be a celebrity game, to be held in Berlin on September 10, in front of 18,000 people! BSB would be playing 'N Sync, another American band popular in Europe (and also managed by the Wright Stuff). The Boys might have been used to singing for that many people, but dribbling and shooting was a different matter altogether.

Naturally, the Boys teased the security crew, on whom they really relied a great deal. But AJ was the worst. Night after night he told them he was going to jump off the stage and land in their arms. And night after night they were ready for him, but he never did it. Finally, in Salzburg, Austria, he was ready to make good on his promise, and came tearing down the ramp to the front of the stage, only to realize he was going too fast, and that, if he jumped, he'd land in the audience!

He tried to stop, but there was water or oil on the stage, and the next view everyone had of AJ was on his butt, legs sticking high in the air, on the edge of the stage! Luckily, there was no damage done, except to his pride, and the security team finally had a good laugh at his expense.

The middle of September brought them home again, for their first "real" American tour, eight dates between the twenty-first and thirtieth of September, including one in New York, before zipping off to Asia for shows in Japan, Manila, Singapore, India, and Hong Kong, the first chance they'd had to thank all the fans there who'd bought their records, a total of well over twelve million copies so far of their two albums, and given them a string of hit singles.

At least, in the middle of October, there would be a

short break, at home in Orlando, where they'd be entertaining on Nickelodeon's *The Big Help,* a show to encourage kids to participate in volunteer activities in their communities, and to thank those who'd done so. Hosted by Melissa Joan Hart, who'd gotten her start on Nickelodeon as Clarissa, before moving on to the big time as *Sabrina the Teenage Witch,* this really was a homecoming show for the Boys. It was at Nickelodeon auditions that AJ, Howie, and Nick had first gotten together. Without the network there might not ever have been BSB! So they sang their hearts out, adding one new song to their set, a cover of the Bill Withers' oldie, ''Lean On Me'' and spent a lot of time greeting everyone who'd come out to see them (and they were the definite star attraction of the show, there was no doubt about that).

BSB were doing very well at home now, very well indeed. ''Quit Playing Games (With My Heart)'' had kept moving smoothly up the chart, all the way to #2, where it was hanging on for its third week. After that it would fall, but not before selling more than a *million* copies, and staying in the Top Fifty for a truly remarkable *nine months*!

And *Backstreet Boys* was matching that, heading all the way up to #4, also going platinum (eventually double platinum!), and sticking around the Top 100 albums for well over six months. There was absolutely no doubt that the Boys had arrived back on their own shores as big stars now.

Then, having just about had time to do their laundry and remind their families that they were real people, not just voices on the other end of a telephone, it was time to hit the road yet again, to start the big world tour. In Spain their performances were supposed to culminate in a big open-air show at Mostenses Plaza in Madrid, the biggest single show they'd ever undertaken, for some 40,000 people. But as the crowd there just kept growing and growing and growing, with people squashed in together, fainting from the heat, the police decreed that it had to be cancelled. There was no way they could guarantee people's safety—even that of the Boys themselves. It was unfortunate, but in the long run, all for the best, no matter how disappointed the fans were. They loved BSB, and the band loved them back, for they agreed that for anyone to risk injury or even death to see them was way over the top.

Late November found them back in Holland, at the Grand Hotel Krasnapolsky in Amsterdam, with a whole group of fans holding a vigil outside, just waiting for them to appear. Not just them, but also the hotel's other guest, bands like Aerosmith, U2, and Hanson, all of them due to drive in Rotterdam that night for the MTV Europe Awards.

Once again, for the second year in a row, Backstreet were up for the MTV Select Award, voted by the viewers, with the Spice Girls (again!), Puff Daddy and Faith Evans, and Hanson for competition. Not only that, they were scheduled to close the show, doing a five-and-a-half minute medley of all their hits for a television audience all across the world—including America. At the end of 1996, they could have seen all this as a dream come true. A year later they'd truly consolidated their position as one of the biggest bands in the entire world, up there with any name in history.

It was an evening when they could mix with names they'd looked up to and listened to growing up, people like Aerosmith's Steve Tyler, and newer stars like Missy Elliott. In company like this, they got what they wanted—respect. The press might have written them off as a boy band, another manufactured unit of cute faces, but they knew there was more to them than that, and their fellow artists treated them as real people.

AJ had seriously hoped that his major crush, Gwen Stefani, the singer for No Doubt, would be there. They

weren't up for any awards themselves, but her boyfriend's band (she dates Gavin Rossdale of Bush) had
been nominated for best rock act—in the end they'd lose
to Oasis.

But there was no losing for Backstreet. As the enve-
lope was opened, manager Johnny Wright turned to AJ
and said, ''Look, the camera's on you! That means
you've got it!'' Poor AJ didn't want to jinx things, and
hid his head his his hands. ''Don't say it until it's true!''
he told Wright.

There was no doubt about it, though. Once again, the
Backstreet Boys were the viewers' choice, absolutely
the biggest band in Europe for 1997.

So when they came back an hour later, to close the
proceedings with a medley of hit singles—seven of them
by now—that had sold millions around the world, it was
with renewed energy and determination. After all this,
people *had* to take them seriously. And that meant
everywhere, even—perhaps particularly—in the U.S.

''I think people will really start to grow up about us,''
B-Rok reflected later that night. ''We're not just a teen
group. We're gonna be around for a *long* time.''

And finally, they were really going to be bringing it
home to America. With both the single and the album
having been major hits, the country was ready. Throughout January and February, they'd be working their way
around the United States.

And starting it all out with a bang, as they played a
one-night show at the place every act hopes to do a
concert—Madison Square Garden, in New York. For
most bands, though, it remained nothing more than a
dream, a goal to aspire to. BSB were playing there as
part of a radio station Christmas party, and starting out
right at the top, now they'd finally brought it all back
home again.

And America was responding, not just in record sales,

but in the crowds. The time was right for them.

"For so long, there was this void of pure pop stuff because of all the alternative acts," JR Ammons of WSTR-FM pointed out in in the *Atlanta Journal and Constitution*. "Now, you're seeing pop acts like the Spice Girls, Hanson, and the Backstreet Boys building audiences."

And it was true. It had taken a long time, but the wheel in America had finally come full circle. There were plenty of reasons for the change, but one of the biggest was that people were just sick and tired of gloom and doom. It had its place, but so did something uplifting and enjoyable. Not to mention that a lot of people (especially parents) didn't like the negative *image* that alternative music enjoyed. Rap had become a thing of the streets, all violence and the degradation of women (at least until Puffy began releasing hits). People wanted something more wholesome, and BSB definitely fit that, without being totally whitebread. At the same time that they were gathering fans by the truckload every day, the Boys understood that they couldn't win over everybody, and accepted that.

"We've come to learn you just can't please everybody," Kevin admits. "We're five guys who love to sing. The five of us believe that destiny has brought us together. And we all feel strongly that we're touching people's lives with our music."

And they were. Everyone who bought the album or the single was touched in some way, they could relate to the emotions behind the songs. The fans screaming for them at Madison Square Garden were touched. This was *their* music, sung to them, written for them, performed by five guys they'd only recently come to know, but already cared about very, very deeply. And that made them important. And it made the fans—the new American fans—equally important to Backstreet. It always has been—and always will be—a two-way street.

But after all that, Canada got to have BSB all to themselves for three weeks. Canadians had been early supporters of the band, the first to make their album triple platinum, and when they'd toured there in 1996, all thirty-two shows had sold out in a staggering twenty minutes. Canada believed, quite rightly, that they were the bomb! Their home video, "Backstreet Boys: The Video," with interviews, television appearances in Europe, and their first five videos, had sold 1.2 *million* copies there! Their two other videos, "Backstreet Boys: Live In Concert" and "Backstreet Boys: Backstreet's Back, Behind the Scenes" weren't far behind that figure. Their reception was like Europe or Asia, but closer to home.

"Canada is definitely our leading market," Kev said before the tour. "We can't believe how incredible it's been there."

And incredible it definitely was. *Backstreet's Back* was double platinum (like the American *Backstreet Boys,* this was an enhanced CD, with video footage and short interviews playable on a computer's CD-ROM drive), and sitting at #8 on the chart, while *Backstreet Boys* was still at #34, having spent over a year in the Top Fifty. The most recent single—in fact, the single they'd released everywhere but America (because "Quit Playing Games (With My Heart)" was still doing so well there)—"As Long As You Love Me," was at #5.

The demand for tickets was so high that they were playing huge venues, and in some places, more than one date. Quebec City would host them on December 29 and Janaury 7. In Montreal they were booked to play a total of *five* dates, December 30, 31, January 1, and January 5 and 6). In Toronto they'd easily sold out the Skydome, home of baseball's Bluejays, with its 27,000 seats. How could it get any bigger than that?

But it was like that every time they were in Canada, and it made them happy to go there often, working their way up to this scale. In Toronto they'd started out at the Warehouse, a mid-sized venue, then returned two months later to sell out Maple Leaf Gardens, where the hockey team played. Now they were well and truly into the big, big time.

This was the same show that had gone over so well in Europe, meant for the arenas they were playing now. It was longer, more elaborate, with plenty of special effects and variety. It was the kind of show the Boys had always hoped they'd be able to stage for their fans. They had the money to make it into a real experience.

One thing the Boys realized was that many of the fans who'd come to see them would be young; that was their fan base. And, however much the band wanted to win over the parents who'd accompany them, a lot would prefer not to be there. So they arranged a "quiet room" next door in the cafe for parents, where they could be away from the noise and be served complimentary coffee, knowing their kids were safe, and close by to meet them after the show.

All the stops had been pulled out on this tour, not just the giant sparklers and incendiary chandeliers, but in terms of the dancing and singing. Backstreet were onstage for more than an hour and a half, finishing with an encore of "Everybody (Backstreet's Back)" which saw them giving everything. But along the way, Brian had appeared solo, accompanying himself on guitar, to sing his song, "That's What She Said," and for "Quit Playing Games (With My Heart)" Kevin had played piano, Nick, drums, and AJ had been on bass, as Brian and Howie sang.

It was apparent, too, that Backstreet were definitely leaning more toward a hip-hop tip now, with frequent raps in the songs. But one thing that hadn't changed was the energy. Every second they were onstage, it was all about the Boys. They danced, they sang, they thanked the audience for their support, and they gave it their all.

The next evening, before traveling back to Montreal for yet another sold-out show in front of 13,000 fans at the Molson Center (meaning they'd end up playing to 65,000 people there!), BSB broadcast a live concert for Much Music, Canada's version of MTV, from its Toronto headquarters.

It was early January in the Great White North, with temperatures well below zero, but that didn't stop fans gathering at 4 A.M. to wait for BSB to appear (and the concert wasn't scheduled until the early evening). Even though the concert had sold out in minutes, still the fans waited. The police had erected barricades, but by noon there were so many people waiting that they had to close off one of Toronto's main thoroughfares, Queen Street, for two blocks, and by three o'clock, girls were regularly being pulled out of the front rows, in danger of being crushed.

By the time the boys appeared, the crowd was one of the largest and most spontaneous the city had seen since Beatlemania in the Sixties. Much Music had erected a giant video screen in the parking lot, but the fans wanted the real thing, and pushed up against the network's windows—their studio was on the ground floor—at Queen and John, yelling "Backstreet Boys!" and "We Want Backstreet!"

It would have been a riot, if the fans hadn't been so well-behaved. As it was, it was still a situation on the edge, particularly when BSB arrived and the show was being broadcast. But once they'd left, everyone went home in an orderly fashion.

The Boys worked their way across Canada, heading slowly westward, wowing audiences wherever they played. Although they were the biggest act to have been in the country for years, mobbed wherever they went, they still tried to make time for the fans, speaking to them, signing autographs for as long as they could, just being exactly what they were at heart, normal, nice guys, who were thrilled and amazed at all the attention they were receiving. Winnipeg, Calgary, Edmonton, all they saw was a winter prairie, until they crossed the moutains and headed down into Vancouver, the last stop on this leg of the tour.

They were tired, but each night of the show was a rush, the screaming, the music, the performance itself. This was why they were doing it, for the sheer love of singing and entertaining. and it was why they'd always be doing it, even in the highly unlikely event of no one going out and buying Backstreet Boys records.

After Vancouver, they needed a break, but there would be none in store for another three months, at least.

Right now, America needed Backstreet pride, and the boys had to give it to them. All over the U.S. copies of *Backstreet Boys* and "Quit Playing Games (With My Heart)" were still flying out of the record stores, but very few people had had the opportunity to see what they could do live. Now, finally, it was time to rectify that, with a blitz of a tour, and plenty of television appearances. America was going to know exacly who the Backstreet Boys were!

1998—AMERICA AND BEYOND

In many ways it was a return to square one. Better than playing the high schools and the malls—well, they were stars now, with an album that was about to turn double platinum in America—but still very far from the superstar status they enjoyed everywhere else, able to sell out giant arenas in minutes.

This would be theaters with capacities of 1,500–2,000 people, and even clubs which could hold fewer people, like the Vanderbilt in Plainview, Long Island, where all the tickets sold out in *four minutes*!

But in America, the truth was that they still weren't big enough for the arena shows. They had to be willing to start from scratch and let the momentum build, and that was exactly what BSB and the Wright Stuff wanted. But selling out all the venues, even the larger ones in the south (like the Bronco Bowl in Dallas) proved to be remarkably easy.

Along with that there'd be plenty of television, which meant that fans with VCRs could set their timers in January to catch the Boys on *The Tonight Show with Jay Leno* and *MTV Live* as well as singing on the telecast of the increasingly prestigious American Music Awards' at the end of the month.

It was hardly the biggest tour Backstreet had undertaken, but certainly one of the most important. It really served to introduce them to all the fans at home who'd gone out and bought their records, and they did it in exactly the same way they'd done it everywhere else, by being willing to work hard and give their all. Record signings, public appearances—they were up for everything. They were accessible, and that was the way they wanted to be, although it was becoming harder as their popularity increased.

It was gratifying to be recognized, after being so anonymous at home for so long, according to Kevin, "but there's the flip side of that, too. The U.S. used to be the only place we had any privacy. We could walk around and not be mobbed. But we're losing that now. People are starting to call our families at home and it's getting a bit scary."

It was the price of fame, and they were willing to pay it—after all, that was why they were focusing all this attention on America! It really looked as though the Backstreet Boys had achieved world domination!

If January seemed busy, it was nothing compared to February, when it looked as if the Backstreet Boys were going to be everywhere. There was Dallas, followed by two radio station concerts in two days, the Vin Del Mar Amphitheater, and the tour closing at the House of Blues in Orlando, home again—but only for a few days, before taking off to spend three days at the San Remo Song Festival, followed by two days of promotion in France, and then two weeks of rehearsals with a new set and new songs for a month in Europe, beginning in Ireland.

That was live. Television saw them performing on ABC's *In Concert* program on February 6, with a guest appearance on the *Ricki Lake* show a week later, followed by Nickelodeon's *All That* on Valentine's Day. For a lot of bands, that would have been enough, but the eighteenth saw them as guests on the *Rosie O'Donnell* show, and the month was rounded out with a cameo on *Sabrina the Teenage Witch*, where they were five anonymous guys fooling around, playing basketball (of course!) in the gym, who accidentally drank Sabrina's talent-in-a-bottle potion and discovered they could magically sing. It was largely uncredited, and the appearance only lasted thirty seconds, but it did give them a chance to sing a capella, one of their real loves, and give a brief rendition of their new single, "As Long As You Love Me," which had been such a massive hit almost everywhere else in the world.

It was all the exposure they could have hoped for, to cement the popularity they'd established. And they'd be back to do plenty more in the coming months. ·

But Europe was calling, yet again, and this tour would be *the* big one! Nothing but the largest venues, taking them all across the Continent over the course of four weeks, beginning with two massive shows in Dublin, Ireland, before heading over to play the NEC in Birmingham, England, followed by two sell-outs at Wembley Arena in London.

From there it was Scandinavia—Denmark, Sweden, and Norway—with a one-day side trip into Germany to tape something that would show them at their very best.

Like MTV, Viva, Germany's music channel, had its own "unplugged" show, and they'd asked Backstreet to come along and tape an edition. For the Boys unplugged meant exactly that; no instruments, no percussion, no tapes, just five voices harmonizing on their material. While they'd done a capella songs in concert, it had been years since they'd performed a whole show that way, and it would be a big test of their abilities, as well as putting a spotlight on a facet of their talents that they really did want to emphasize. Naturally, there'd be plenty of ballads in there, but they could do their up-tempo material, too, as well of some of the sly covers they'd managed to slip in over the years—"Betcha By

Golly Wow," "End of the Road," and the other songs they'd sung for practice when they first got together. It would be almost like turning the clock back, except that this time they'd be performing for millions of viewers instead of a couple of executives in a record company lobby. Time had moved along, and it was quite definitely on their side.

After the date in Germany, it would be back to the rigor of concerts, with two days in Sweden, before a week in Holland, Belgium, and France, and the tour culminating in four Spanish dates, all at sports palaces, finishing April 13 in Madrid.

In twenty-seven days they'd play a total of twenty-one shows, in front of almost a million fans. It was going to be quite an event. Funnily, though, it would be quite as grueling as many tours they'd undertaken; in several places they were playing more than one date at a venue, which meant less road time, and the crew wouldn't have to tear down and rebuild the set, which had become more and more extensive. Still, it was a hectic schedule.

The Boys might be huge, but they were still willing to go into radio stations, answer questions, talk to DJs and fans. For them, it was the only way to be, to keep communicating with people, to stay close to their fans.

Too many bands had made the mistake of putting distance and barriers between themselves and their fans, and it was something Backstreet was never going to let happen. For their own physical safety, there had to be limits, but they still wanted to be as accessible.

Not just the touring, but also the endless promotion was exhausting, but worth it. Although, as Howie points out, their lives are different from the way most people imagine.

"It does involve a little bit of work," he says. "You would think the lifestyle of an entertainer means always doing shows, partying after work, then getting up to do a show the next day. That's not really so. But it's good; we don't mind this kind of lifestyle. Just as long as we are keeping busy.''

There seems to be no danger of them not being busy, at least in the forseeable future! But after Europe they'll have two whole weeks off before Backstreet will be back in the Orlando house. Over the course of two weeks they'll be playing five times at the Magic Kingdom Grad Nights at Disneyworld. For Kev, in particular, it'll be a return to old haunts, the place he worked until he joined BSB. And for those graduates who'll be attending, it'll be the perfect seal on four years of high school memories.

The Boys will find it an easy series of shows. No traveling, other than to and from home, just a short drive, and after two weeks of having nothing (!) to do, the concerts will probably be a welcome change, and a chance to keep their voices and moves in shape before they hit the road again on Memorial Day, playing the KISS 108 Party in Boston, the start of another trek across America.

One thing no one can deny is that they've worked very hard for their success. They've *earned* it. Each of them came into this with a dream, and they found that by working together they could make it into a reality. Not only that, but they could have fun doing it!

Perhaps none of them expected it to take off the way it has, that they'd be on posters on countless bedroom walls, or such huge international stars—dreams rarely go quite that far. But it's happened, and the Backstreet pride is going to be alive for a long, long time.

Inevitably, where there's love, there's also hate, and while Backstreet might have generated more than 100 fan sites, there have also been two anti-BSB sites started on the Web. Not that they mind. In fact, a fan printed up the material from one of those sites and gave it to them. ''. . . [W]e found it quite entertaining,'' Kevin laughs. "You can't please everybody, so you just gotta laugh at these kinds of things."

That sites like that would happen was almost inevitable (both the Spice Girls and Hanson have them, too, but in cyberspace free speech rules). But virtually all the sites dedicated to them are from real fans. There's the official site, naturally, with all the information about upcoming shows all over the world, but it's the fan sites that are the most interesting, to see just how much some people love them, collecting pictures, interviews, articles, sound clips, and all manner of things about them.

Cuddly Nick seems to be the slight favorite among site owners in terms of space, but there's really little to choose between any of the five. They may be all individuals, but as a whole they're far stronger than they could ever be apart.

To see America finally catch up with the phenomenon (and make no mistake, the Backstreet Boys *are* a phenomenon) is particularly gratifying for those who saw them the first time around, when they started out playing those high schools and malls and wondered whatever happened to them. These days they're all over the teen magazines, vying with Hanson for cover space. There's an official Backstreet Boys magazine that's selling like crazy in the stores, not to mention booklets, and, in particular, poster booklets. There's a newsgroup on the Internet just about them.

And, of course, there are the T-shirts, baseball caps, keychains, posters, and even boxer shorts with the Backstreet logo and pictures of the Boys. Those, too, are selling by the truckload, and not just at their shows.

The truth is, people want their BSB. It's a musical thing, but it's gone way beyond the sound of five voices working together, five guys dancing onstage or in a video. They've become icons to a generation, and there's nothing wrong with that at all. Every generation *needs* its icons.

There's even one in the Backstreet family coming up for the next generation—Nick's little brother, Aaron. He was with them in Hawaii on their band vacation, and has opened shows for them in Europe.

He's even released his first CD, *Aaron Carter,* which features Nick on backing vocals on one track, and the first single from it, a remake of the old pop song "Crush On you" went into the charts in Germany.

If that all sounds too bizarre, it's not. It's not a case of cashing in on the Backstreet fame. Aaron, who's ten now (born December 7, 1987), put his first band together when he was seven, with three classmates, going out under the name Dead End, to play local libraries and coffeehouses. They stayed together for three years.

Sure, he was inspired by his older brother, but that didn't mean Aaron had no talent; quite the opposite. He began working with a vocal coach, and once the Boys and the Wrights heard him, they knew he had that magical ingredient for stardom. At four foot five and sixty-five pounds, he might still be small to be onstage, but there's no doubting the reception he's received opening for BSB. Of course, the fact that he looks just like a smaller version of Nick hasn't hurt things one bit. But Aaron is talented in his own right, and might even in time—who knows?—end up as a star in his own right.

That's all for the future. But there's a lot to look ahead to. The Backstreet Boys as we know and love them will remain exactly as they are. It's the chemistry of those five particular voices and personalities that make them so special. If one member left, they would never attempt to replace him. There simply wouldn't be BSB any more.

That's unlikely; why would any of them want to leave? But over the course of the next few months they might all want to do solo albums. That's *quite* possible. Kev, Brian, AJ, Howie, and Nick *are* all individuals, with different ideas to express. In fact, Kev says,

". . . [W]e'd like to do what New Edition did. They all went their separate ways and had solo careers and then got back together and put out more hits."

There's absolutely no reason why, in the long run, that shouldn't be possible. But time will tell, as always.

Closer to the present, there are plenty of projects besides concerts and albums in hand. Nick is still talking very enthusiastically about his comic book idea, and that is very likely to happen, with, Nick explains, "each of us developing a power, like mutants, and battling a group of aliens who are trying to take over the world through music."

And there's all manner of marketing offers being thrown at the boys—television cartoons, bedsheets, even dolls, but they're very dubious about all that exploitation. Another idea that's being explored is a movie (and why not? *Spiceworld* has done pretty well). That makes a lot of sense. With the exception of Brian, all the rest of Backstreet have plenty of acting experience. In fact, each of them has already been approached about acting roles, which so far they've resolutely turned down to concentrate on their musical career. But a movie with all of them in it could be very attractive, given the right script and, of course, the time to do it properly.

Logically, it would be the next step. As a band, they can only be in so many places, and as much as they love the rush of performing, there are only so many concerts they can stage in a year—never enough to satisfy the fans they now have all over the world. A movie would allow them to be everywhere at once, and fans could see them in close up, hear them speak, watch them sing and dance (it would, after all, be impossible to imagine a BSB movie without any singing or dancing!), and a Backstreet Boys movie would be the perfect way to greet the millennium.

So where does it all go from here? Only bigger and better, if you can believe that. In America, people now know their names, and who they are. On TV, they're brought in to increase the ratings during the semi-annual sweeps period—just look at the way they were all over television in February 1998, one of those very sweeps periods. Their album has gone double platinum, with over two million copies sold, while "Quit Playing Games (With My Heart)" simply won't leave the charts, even as the next single, "As Long As You Love Me" is ready to go and take its place. It might not be like Europe or Canada or Asia yet, but it's getting there. And that means even more touring, all across the country, to give fans a chance to see what they're like.

Already, the collection of their early videos has been released here, the same collection that sold 1.2 million copies in Canada, and could well repeat that feat here. And on the same day, Jive also came out with their "Live In Concert" video, a little dated now, since it was recorded in Germany at the end of 1996, but still a sample of what they're like onstage for all the American fans who haven't had a chance to see them yet.

In Canada, Europe, and Asia, of course, it's only going to get more and more difficult to see them. The demand for Backstreet is so high that only the largest venues are big enough, and even those can only hold so many fans. Which is why they're playing multiple nights on this tour, and in the future it's quite possible that they'll have to do several nights at massive domes and stadiums, just to satisfy all the people who want to see them.

If it works out like that, or when they sell out Madison Square Garden for three nights in a row, more power to them. Along with a couple of other bands, they've been responsible for bringing back pop music, for letting harmony ring. They've followed their dreams, from the difficult times to the smooth, and believed in themselves and what they were doing every step and note of the way. So it's only right that Backstreet rules now.

♪ THE LAST PART ♪

"**W**e're for real," says Howie-D, and you know that's got to be true. It's the only way Backstreet could have become so huge everywhere. Anyone can manufacture a group, and people have accused BSB of being manufactured, but in this case it's just so ridiculous.

These are five talented guys who came together on their own with absolutely no guarantee of success, who began singing because they loved it. When Howie met AJ, and then Nick joined in on harmony, there was nothing manufactured about that. Even when Kevin, and then Brian were drafted in to replace the members who hadn't worked out, that wasn't fake. It all came together because the chemistry was there. They sang so well together, they could move together, they thought alike ... that's what makes Backstreet so special. And it's why they've got the Backstreet pride. They've never been frightened of hard work.

Long hours and lots of miles were what they needed to make it even begin to happen, long before there was any chance of a record hitting the charts, before they even had a contract with Jive.

They've always been in this for the long haul. You're not going to get rich and famous touring high schools and malls. What you will do is get experience, make friends, win fans, and do it the hard way, the real way, a way that lasts for years.

When they sang in 1995 that they'd had it going on for years, that was no lie. From April 7, 1993, when Brian arrived in Florida and first sang with the others, it had been going on. That was their story.

The slow start, the build up to it all only helped them. By the time "We've Got It Goin' On" smashed the charts in Germany, they were already seasoned, used to performing in front of audiences, entertaining. They'd lived and worked together for two years as a unit, they were used to each other. More important, they were ready and hungry for that next move, and they weren't likely to crack under the strain—actually, it was less strain than they had, staying in better hotels, being treated better. Like any group, they'd paid their dues when their time came around.

They had an opportunity, and they took it. America wasn't interested, so they took BSB on the road and pursued fame; they made the sensible decision. They grew up together as they went around Europe and Asia, as they recorded their second album, and played arenas all over.

That meant, when they brought it all back home again, when America was finally ready for some Backstreet magic, they were mature, capable of doing everything that needed to be done. At eighteen, Nick is more mature than most college freshmen. He's seen things most people won't see in their whole lives. He's literally been all around the world, stood up in front of thousands and thousands of people at a time, played drums for them. And AJ, Kevin, Brian, and Howie have all become men in the last two years.

The things that haven't changed in any of them, though, are the important qualities, the ones that make them who they are. They're all still humble, knowing that beyond talent, a part of success is luck. They know full well who put them where they are—their fans. And they're grateful for that. Backstreet have never gone in for star trips. As much as they can, they're happy to spend time with the fans, to sign autographs, to talk to them—in AJ's case, even to call them.

For them, being famous isn't about limousines, high living, money, or power. It's about responsibility. A responsibility to be available to the people who put them there. That's why, when fans have visited (back in the days when European magazines went so far as to print their home addresses), they were always courteous and kind to the people who'd put them where they are today. Not just the Boys themselves, but their families were, too, letting strangers into their homes, treating them with generosity and respect.

One feature of *every* Backstreet Boys show is them saying thank you. The hype is out there—let's face it, it's hard not to get an ego when you have thousands of girls screaming your name. But they've always kept their feet very firmly planted on the ground. Part of that is their upbringing. All five of the Boys were raised right, as they readily admit. But another part, maybe the bigger part, is just the way they are. These are five genuinely nice guys, no pose, no front, just seriously good people. They're grateful for the success. They don't see it as their right, their just reward. They know that it's a fine line between success and failure, and they're glad to have landed on the right side of it. Without you—the people buying this book, the people who've bought their records and gone to their shows—it wouldn't have all been going on for years at all. You're the people they've sung to, the people who've kept them going when they've been so tired after endless weeks on the road. Even if it can't be as personal as it once was, simply because of the bigger crowds, the greater and greater demands on their time, that doesn't mean they've forgotten. Every day is a lesson to them. At every show, when the teddy bears hit the stage (and they're all donated to charity, by the way), each one is a reminder.

All the days that have gone before, every high school and mall, every recording session, every appearance on television, and in particular every single show, they've all been for you. You're what it's all about for them. You make everything worthwhile. They give you their all, and you give it right back to them.

Kevin, Howie, Brian, AJ, and Nick—the Backsreet Boys—thank you for everything.

DISCOGRAPHY

AMERICA

Singles

"We've Got It Goin' On"—1995
"Quit Playing Games (With My Heart)"—1997
"As Long As You Love Me"—1998

Albums

BACKSTREET BOYS (Enhanced CD)
We've Got It Goin' On—Quit Playing Games (With My Heart)—
As Long As You Love Me—Everybody (Backstreet's Back)—
All I Have To Give—Anywhere For You—Hey, Mr. DJ (Keep
Playin' This Song)—I'll Never Break your Heart—Darlin'—Get
Down (You're The One For Me)—Set Adrift On Memory Bliss—
If You Want It To Be Good Girl (Get Yourself A Bad Boy)

Videos

Backstreet Boys—The Video
Backstreet Boys—Live In Concert

EUROPE, ASIA

Singles

"We've Got It Goin' On"—1995 (re-released in Britain, 1996)
"Get Down (You're The One For Me)"—1996
"I'll Never Break Your Heart"—1996
"Quit Playing Games (With My Heart)"—1996
"Anywhere For You"—1997
"Everybody (Backstreet's Back)"—1997
"As Long As You Love Me"—1997
"All I Have To Give"—1998

Albums

BACKSTREET BOYS

We've Got It Goin' On—Anywhere For You—Get Down (You're The One For Me)—I'll Never Break Your Heart—Quit Playing Games (With My Heart)—Boys Will Be Boys—Just To Be Close To You—I Wanna Be With You—Every Time I Close My Eyes—Darlin' Let's Have A Party—Roll With It—Nobody But You—Don't Leave Me (+ 2 live tracks)

BACKSTREET'S BACK

Everybody (Backstreet's Back)—As Long As You Love Me—All I Have To Give—Missing You—That's The Way I Like It—10,000 Promises—Like A Child—Hey, Mr. DJ (Keep Playin' This song)—Set Adrift On Memory Bliss—That's What She Said—If You Want It To Be Good Girl (Get yourself A Bad Boy—All I Have To Give (Part II—The Conversation Mix)—If I Don't Have You

Videos

Backstreet Boys—The Video
Backstreet Boys—Live In Concert
Backstreet Boys—Backstreet's Back: Behind The Scenes

CANADA

Singles

As Europe and Asia

Albums

BACKSTREET BOYS

We've Got It Goin' On—Get Down (You're The One For Me)—I'll Never Break Your Heart—Quit Playing Games (With My Heart)—Boys Will Be Boys—Just To Be Close To You—I Wanna Be With You—Every Time I Close My Eyes—Darlin'—Roll With It

BACKSTREET'S BACK

Everybody (Backstreet's Back)—As Long As You Love Me—All I Have to Give—That's The Way I Like It—10,000 Prom-

ises—Like A Child—Hey, Mr. DJ (Keep Playin' This Song)—
Set Adrift On Memory Bliss—That's What She Said— Any-
where For You—If You Want It To Be Good Girl (Get
Yourself A Bad Boy)—If I Don't Have You

Videos

As Europe and Asia

THE BACKSTREETS OF THE INTERNET

If you have a computer, you can spend hours checking out the
World Wide Web for the 411 on the Boys. With over 100 sites,
there are plenty of places to point your browser. Some are
good, some pretty skinny.

One place you *really* need to check is the official web site
(http://www.backstreetboys.com), which will keep you totally up
to date about what's going on in the Backstreet world, right
down to where they'll be playing months from now—so you
can really plan ahead.

Beyond that, two sites that really stand out can be found at:
http://www.geocities.com/SunsetStrip/Towers/3717/index.html
and
http://www.geocities.com/SunsetStrip/Studio/3106/

TIMELINE

1972	
3 October	Kevin Richardson born, Lexington, KY.
1973	
22 August	Howard Dwayne Dorough born, Orlando, FL.
1975	
20 February	Brian Thomas Littrell born, Lexington, KY.
1978	
9 January	Alexander James McLean born.
1980	
28 January	Nicholas Gene Carter born, Jamestown, NY.
	Brian almost dies of a heart infection.
1990	
	Kevin moves to Orlando.
1991	
August 26	Kevin's father dies of cancer.
1993	
January	Howie, AJ, and Nick begin singing together.
March	Kevin joins the band to replace two members who didn't work out.
April 7	Brian flies to Florida, auditions, and the Backstreet Boys are born.
1994	
	BSB sign a deal with Mercury Records, and end up being dropped.
	BSB sign with Jive Records.

1995

> BSB record in Sweden with Denniz PoP, then in Orlando.

Summer
> "We've Got It Goin' On" released in U.S.—rises to #69.

Fall
> Single is a hit in Germany, Canada and all over Europe.
>
> BSB tour Europe for the first time.
>
> Tour with PJ and Duncan in England.

1996

January
> Voted *Smash Hits* Best Newcomers of the Year.

Spring
> BSB's first Canadian appearance at Place Vertu Mall in Montreal draws 3,000 fans.
>
> BSB make video for "Get Down (You're The One For Me)".
>
> Named Best Newcomer in Britain's Red Nose Awards.
>
> "Get Down (You're The One For Me)" released, a hit in Canada and Europe.
>
> BSB begin a 35-city European tour.
>
> Make videos for "Quit Playing Games (With My Heart)" and "I'll Never Break Your Heart."

August
> BSB play Festival des Montgolsieres in Quebec to 65,000 people.

September/October
> *Backstreet Boys* released in Europe, Canada, and Asia. Goes gold or platinum in over 30 countries.
>
> "Anywhere For You" issued as a single in Asia.

November
> "I'll Never Break Your Heart" released as a European single.

December
> BSB receive the MTV Select Award in Europe.
>
> BSB tour Germany. Concert in Frankfurt shown on Premiere TV, later released as a

home video, "Back Street Boys: Live In Concert."

"Christmas Time" released to fan club.

1997

January
"Quit Playing Games (With My Heart)" released.

BSB receive *Smash Hits* Award for Best Roadshow.

BSB tour Canada.

February
Relax for eight days in Hawaii.

"Anywhere For You" released as a single in Europe.

Return to Orlando to begin recording for *Backstreet's Back*.

May/June
BSB tour Europe, culminating in a sold-out show at England's Wembley Arena on June 26.

Fly to Los Angeles to make videos for "As Long As You Love Me," "All I Have To Give" and "Everybody (Backstreet's Back)."

"Quit Playing Games (With My Heart) released in the U.S. as a single.

July
Single enters the *Billboard* Hot 100 at #24; it will rise to #2.

The American version of *Backstreet Boys* is released. It will go all the way to #4.

"Everybody (Backstreet's Back)" released in Canada, Asia, and Europe, enters the chart in the Top Ten in 10 countries.

August
BSB start their first European stadium tour.

Backstreet's Back released everywhere but America.

September 18
BSB play charity all-star basketball game in Berlin, Germany.

BSB undertake their first U.S. tour, eight dates only.

October	Entertain on Nickelodeon's *The Big Help*.
	Both "Quit Playing Games (With My Heart)" and *Backstreet Boys* are certified platinum in America. The album will go double platinum.
	European tour. Date in Spain cancelled when too many people try to get into the venue.
November	Receive MTV Select Award for the second year.
December	Play Madison Square Garden in New York.
	Begin Canadian tour, playing five dates in Montreal, and sell out the Skydome in Toronto.
1998	
January	Tape a concert for Much Music in Toronto. The crush of fans forces police to close streets.
	Finish Canadian tour, begin American dates. On *The Tonight Show with Jay Leno* and *MTV Live*.
February	Continue American dates. Appear on *The Rosie O'Donnell Show* and *Sabrina the Teenage Witch*.
	Conclude American tour 21st in Orlando.
March 17	Begin European tour in Dublin, Ireland.
March 28	Record "Viva Unplugged" in Germany.
April 13	Conclude European tour in Madrid, Spain.
April-May	Appear at Magic Kingdom Grad Nights, Orlando, FL.